Words at Work

Words at Work
Lectures on Textual Structure

Randolph Quirk
President of the British Academy

Longman

Longman Group UK Limited,
Longman House, Burnt Mill, Harlow,
Essex CM20 2JE, England
and Associated Companies throughout the world.

Words at Work was first published in 1986 by Singapore University
Press

Longman edition first published 1986

ISBN 0–582–00120–X

Printed by Fong & Sons Printers Pte. Ltd.

Contents

Preface

During a period of two months in late 1985 and early 1986, I was privileged to enjoy residence in Singapore with appointment as Lee Kuan Yew Distinguished Visitor. In addition to numerous addresses before groups as various as the Singapore Association for Applied Linguistics, the Singapore Society of Editors, the staff of the *Straits Times*, postgraduates of the Regional Language Centre (RELC), students and staff of the English Department of the National University of Singapore, I gave eight public lectures on 'The Nature and Constituents of Textual Structure'.

In selecting the topic of discourse and textual structure for these special lectures in Singapore, I had in mind the repeated emphasis by the Prime Minister himself on the importance of communicative skills (particularly in English and Mandarin) for Singapore's multilingual society, located at so crucially nodal a geographical point for international commerce. I had in mind also an address delivered in London at the Royal Society in July 1983 by Dr Goh Keng Swee (then Deputy Prime Minister of Singapore), and published the same year by the Trade Policy Research Centre as *Public Administration and Economic Development in LDCs*. In this, Dr Goh set out guidelines for developing countries which included 'investment in human beings' through excellence of education; and the 'careful study, diligent application and intelligent adjustment' of Western models. The study of communication models must doubtless be of prime relevance in this connection, but I venture to hope that such relevance extends far beyond Southeast Asia.

The present book therefore offers a somewhat generalised version of my Singapore lectures, and one that has been revised in the light of the extremely valuable contributions made by members of the audience during the discussion period after each lecture. Those who have thus influenced much-needed changes and improvements are too numerous for me to acknowledge my debt to them by name, but I must make an exception in the case of Mrs Lee Sow Ling whose searching comments, along with those of my wife, have been particularly pervasive and welcome.

My debt goes far beyond my audiences, however, and I take this opportunity of thanking the authorities of the National University of Singapore — especially the Vice-Chancellor, Professor Lim Pin; the Dean of Arts and Social Sciences, Professor Edwin Thumboo; and the Director of the University Liaison Office, Mr Peter Lim — for enabling me to come to Singapore and for making my stay so enjoyable and so intellectually stimulating.

Randolph Quirk
London
June 1986

Lecture One
Basics of Communication

For all the scientific panoply involved in the description of communication and for all the modern electronic advances in creating more effective channels for communication, the greatest and most abiding difficulty about human communication is that it is human. And in this too lie its subtlety, its value, and its limitless potentiality: in considering it, we must ever bear in mind human frailty — whether of mind or morale — as well as human creativity. Every time we attempt to communicate, every time we attempt to interpret and understand someone else's communication, we are engaged in the uncertain and risky task of inference.

Inference. We can never *know*. Every time we speak, we are obliged to make guesses about what our hearer knows and about how he or she (and it often matters which) will relate that knowledge to what we want to say. Let me give a simple example — if only to show that examples are rarely simple:

Becker beat McEnroe in straight sets.

Clearly, this statement assumes a knowledge of tennis in the hearer: otherwise the expression 'in straight sets' would be meaningless. Yet the communication will not become less demanding if we paraphrase the technical expression and say

Becker beat McEnroe decisively

since this still assumes a knowledge of tennis; otherwise Becker and McEnroe could be boxers or sprinters or chess-players or candidates in a political election. More narrowly, the communication assumes an *up-to-date* knowledge of *international* tennis, since it is only after Wimbledon 1985 that the sentence achieves plausibility in the real world. Seen from this point of view, we note that as a piece of *communication* the sentence has a very real 'value-added' meaning, as compared with the mere grammatical and lexical

9

meaning, the abstract *linguistic* meaning of what we might regard as a strictly comparable sentence:

Jack beat Jill in straight sets.

Whether we meet this last example in an English textbook or whether we hear it said of a real-world, but unknown, 'Jack' and 'Jill', the meaning depends only on understanding that a tennis match comprises sets and if all sets are won by one side, that side can be said to have beaten the other 'in straight sets'. The original communication, plausible as I say only since August 1985, has a very different real meaning in the real world: an earlier virtually unbeatable champion, McEnroe, has been beaten by a young man who was hitherto virtually unknown. The meaning is a momentous change in the world of first-class tennis.

I have laboured this so-called 'simple' example to make one basic point: that in communication, we have an essential correlation between a semiotic system (in the present context, largely the English language) and an independently existent world (in the present context, a system of shared knowledge, myth, or belief — including a willingly suspended disbelief: as in fiction). Without that correlation, there can be no communication. The sentence

Both my son's flointles have died recently

has a perfect grammatical structure but is not a communication since no hearer knows what a *flointle* is. Equally, however,

Both my son's parents have died recently

is no communication since, although this time the faultless grammar is accompanied by no unknown words, there can be no correlation between the sentence and any situation in the real world or in any plausible fictive one.[1]

On the semiotic side of the correlation, I said that for our purposes we were largely concerned with the English language. Before I come to consider the qualification 'largely', let me expand a little on what the English language embraces. Lexicon obviously. The effectiveness of every communication depends on the selection

---

[1] The fact we might 'read' a meaning into either sentence (for example, imagining the son to be adopted in the second) serves only to endorse the co-operative principle discussed below.

of specific lexical items from the hundreds of thousands that are available to us as speakers and writers. Our word stock can be seen as constituting a central core of general purpose items like *street, hand, top, arrange, fetch, heavy, bright, always* (which are virtually indispensable, regardless of the nature of the communication), surrounded by a vast array of words with more specialised reference like *chromosome, appendix, instigate, affirmative*. The latter enable us to articulate communications with great precision for such purposes as legal definition and scientific description, where our reliance on the assumed shared knowledge between the relatively few competent participants is all the greater. But less momentous topics than law and science have their technical vocabulary — we have seen an instance in the tennis report 'X beat Y in straight sets', and this example is useful in another respect. It draws our attention to the fact that words belong to the core or to the surrounding areas of specialisation not as formal items but in respect of their meanings. Thus *straight* and *set* belong to the common core when used in the senses understood in the sentences

> She drew a *straight* line on the page.
>
> The child has a fine *set* of teeth.

But both words are used in special senses outside the common core when applied to tennis in the expression *straight sets*. And this, we notice, while preserving the grammatical relations of the items: *straight* an adjective, *set* a noun. When a formal item is used in two different grammatical functions, it is still commoner to find these in different domains of the lexicon: 'I caught the bird with a *net*', 'The company has made a *net* profit'. 'Every time he plays Bartok, his wife *plugs* her ears', 'The car wouldn't start because the *plugs* were wet'.

No less than with lexicon, the choices of *grammar* crucially affect any communication we attempt. A noun phrase of high density that may seem admirable as we seek to express ourselves with careful precision may utterly confuse the reader or listener even if it appears in sentence-final position:

> As the advance contingent emerged from forest cover, a burst of hostile fire destroyed *the newly repaired armour-plated off-side front wing of the senior commander's light single-turreted patrol vehicle on which was mounted the experimental range-finder.*

A communicator more sympathetic to his audience and determined to get his message across would avoid packing so much information into a single noun phrase, even if this meant making the report lengthier. Perhaps something like this:

> It had been decided to mount the experimental range-finder on the senior commander's patrol vehicle. This was of the single-turreted type with armour-plated front wings. The off-side one had been newly repaired and seemed a good place for the range-finder. But this was precisely the part that was destroyed by a burst of hostile fire as the advance contingent emerged from forest cover.

Here more than sixty words are used where less than forty appeared in the earlier version; seven clauses where three had served before. There can be no doubt that the second is clearer and that it communicates faster despite its greater prolixity. And the difference lies solidly in grammar, not lexicon. Both versions have all the lexical items presents in the first, and the second adds few though it repeats some. Although in many cases the re-working of a message for greater efficiency involves lexical choices, in many we are concerned with grammatical choices: how many clauses, what structure of clauses, whether to use the active or the passive, which parts to pronominalise, which parts to front or postpone, which device to use in order to move constituents to where we want them.

The grammar of English provides a rich array of such choices (cf Halliday, 1985) and the two versions of a single message that I have given could be supplemented by an indefinitely large selection of further alternatives. No one should underestimate the importance of taking time to exploit to the full the lexical and grammatical resources at our disposal as we sensitively feel out the best way of getting our message across in the particular circumstances. These will include whether, at one extreme, we are speaking face to face with hearers we know and who can at once ask for clarification, or whether, at the other extreme, we are writing for unknown readers whose comprehension we have to guess. But irrespective of such variables, there are general maxims of lexical selection and grammatical organisation, as we shall see in the course of these lectures (cf also Cole and Morgan, 1975; Hoey, 1983; Nash, 1980; Schenkein, 1978). One is to ensure that we start from as secure a position as possible in assessing the shared knowledge of speaker and hearer: and then of proceeding from the relatively well-known, established, 'given' to the relatively unknown, unfamiliar, new. Thus in both versions of the military example, I have assumed a prior knowledge of the experimental range-finder. If I had been in some doubt, my second version might have begun:

> There had been, as you may know, some experiments
> to devise a different type of range-finder.

If I was fairly sure I was on new ground, on the other hand, my opening might have been more starkly:

> There had been some experiments to devise a different
> type of range-finder.

And if I felt my hearer knew nothing about guns, I would take a further step back, perhaps with something like this:

> One of the difficulties in shooting is to establish the
> distance between the gun and the target; this is called
> 'finding the range'. There had been some experiments
> to devise a different type of range-finder ...

But I have been speaking as though a written version of a communication was identical with its spoken version. It is not, of course. Speech has audible features such as intonation, relative loudness, tempo and rhythm which have no one-for-one correlate in the English writing system. Because even the most literate of us do more than ninety-nine per cent of our communicating in speech, we find written communication far harder to cope with, whether we are doing the writing or whether we are at the receiving end as readers. As writers, we tend to forget that our readers (especially if they are strangers who do not know us personally) cannot easily reconstruct the intonation or stress or rhythm from what we have written: though for us, hearing our own speech mentally as we write, it may seem easy enough. As readers, on the other hand, we tend to vocalise (actually or in imagination) our own version of the inferred intonation and stress and rhythm in what we read, without mentally standing back to wonder how the writer would have sounded if he had spoken aloud what he has written for us.

So it is that I may write:

> The law insists that taxis only pick up passengers in
> this street

and because I am confident that anyone would have known exactly what I meant if I had said it aloud, I am foolish or inconsiderate enough to believe that it is equally clear to any reader in its written version. But in fact I would have said it in one of at least three ways (cf Taglicht, 1984). One would have meant:

> The law insists that it is *only taxis* that may pick up passengers in this street (private cars, for example, are forbidden to stop here).

Another would have meant:

> The law insists that taxis may *only pick up* passengers: they are not allowed to discharge passengers in this street.

A third version would have meant:

> The law insists that taxis use *this street alone* for picking up passengers: they are not allowed to do so in neighbouring streets.

But just as in writing I have failed to anticipate that the sentence has other than the meaning I had in mind, so readers may equally not recognise the sentence as ambiguous: they may just impose their own meaning upon it, convinced that they understand, though in fact they have only about one chance in three of having selected the correct one. And of course, as writers and readers, we are *doubly* disadvantaged: the writing system obliges us to compensate for absent phonological features and simultaneously debars us from the instantaneous check for understanding that is possible when we are in the normal face-to-face situation of spoken discourse. So it is that we have the paradox: though writing and reading constitute only a miniscule fraction of human communication, they require a totally disproportionate amount of learning, practice, skill and sympathetic attention.

So far I have referred to writing in respect to the ways in which it is deficient as compared with spoken communication: reasonably enough, since they are certainly the greatest source of difficulty. But the deficiencies are not all on one side. Writing has features that are absent from speech. For example, in writing, there is a clear distinction between capital letters and small letters, between apostrophe *s* and plural *s*, between roman type and italics, indeed between one word and another. A lecture title read over the telephone as:

> Some art in sound

was taken down by a stenographer as

> Sir Martin's hound

and we have to admit that, in isolation, neither was obviously less plausible than the other. But in written transmission no such confusion could have occured. Again, there is a great deal of difference between

> Give me the racing news, please

and

> Give me *The Racing News*, please

though in speech they sound identical. There is the story of the customer who said to an assistant in a bookstore:

> I've come for T.S. Eliot's *Family Reunion*

and received the puzzled reply:

> Well, I don't think it's being held here, madam.

With its access to such symbols as question marks and quotation marks, writing also makes sharp distinctions that can be blurred into ambiguity in speech. This is true even of such pairs as the following, where intonation need not always distinguish one from the other:

> 1(a) Was he tired!
> (b) Was he tired?

> 2(a) John is not coming, then.
> (b) John is not coming, then?

> 3(a) The doctor said I need a holiday.
> (b) The doctor said, 'I need a holiday'.

There are other visual codes within the graphic system, some of them well-established international conventions like the use of

'Gothic' black-letter typeface for the title of a newspaper:

Fig. 1

or more casual *ad hoc* devises where — in London, for example — a sign like this outside a restaurant:

Fig. 2

is to be interpreted as 'good *Greek* food'.

Clearly, we would find it difficult in speech to match such instances of *double entendre* — or perhaps I should say the *double voir*. Just as able speakers exploit the subtleties available through intonation and other oral features absent from writing, so the alert writer is quick to use features of the graphic system that are without oral correlates. In the fourth lecture we shall discuss Updike's *I/eye* and Jacobson's *annalist/analyst*, but one does not need to go to sophisticated fiction. The phenomenon is commonplace in the puns and witticisms of smart journalism, which require both phonic realisation and visual cues operating simultaneously to produce the desired effect. In *The Guardian* of 9 November 1985, an article on European holiday resorts was headed

Savoie Fare

Here the spelling has to be interpreted in terms of travel (*fare*) to the Haute-Savoie region of France, but the sound suggests simultaneously *savoir faire* as this is informally pronounced in English, an expression appropriately redolent both of France and of sophisticated taste. But if one had heard the article read aloud without seeing it, only the *savoir faire* sense would have been communicated — and rather mystifyingly at that.

With this example and its dependence on the European scene

(not to mention the tastes of *Guardian* readers), we clearly reach out beyond the limits of the language side of the correlation I specified earlier: beyond language, that is, to the pragmatic conditions that subsist in shared knowledge. In spoken language, such limits are often acknowledged by the need for non-linguistic accompaniment such as the smile of apology, of encouragement, of self-deprecation, of conspiracy to jest; the raised eyebrow, the hunch of shoulders, the spread of fingers, the shaping gesture of hands and arms.

Or of course we may point to an actual example or a diagrammatic representation of an example. In most real discourse in the real world, language is accompanied by visual aids of this kind; it is exceptional to be talking in the dark, literally or figuratively. Yet even so, what we select from these visual accompaniments, whether as emitters or receivers of communication, continues to depend upon shared knowledge. There is in London an employment agency, now with branches in many places but bearing the name of the street in which it started up: the Brook Street Bureau. The firm seeks to persuade those seeking work to register with them and it seeks equally to persuade employers that this is where they will get the best staff. On the London Underground there has been an advertising campaign exploiting with elegant economy the rhetorical polar contrast: 'Not that, but this', 'Avoid that, choose this'. The economy resides in two contrasting pictures, each with a brief contrasting caption. For example, two vases of tulips, the one well-tended, the other neglected (Fig. 3). If you hire an assistant

Sloppy girl   Brook Street girl

Fig. 3

from any other agency, she is liable to be sloppy: not so, if you hire from a branch of Brook Street. But this contrast is expressed only very indirectly by means of the words: the opposite of 'sloppy' is merely implied by 'Brook Street', partly by the rhetorical expectation of contrast rather than (say) paraphrase, partly by what have been selected as contrasting 'icons' of *sloppy* and *Brook Street*. Successful interpretation depends on the relatively minor cultural feature that office desks are often decorated by a vase of flowers, and a glance at how well those flowers are tended will suggest how alert and efficient the desk's occupant is. Here we have a notable example of that reliance on inference which I stressed at the outset.

But Brook Street handles male staff as well as female staff, and an advertisement with similar contrastive momentum can also be seen on the Underground (Fig. 4). This is somewhat more ambitious, with the allusion to H.G. Wells' scientific fiction in the 'invisible man', which for the purposes of the implied contrast we must be prepared to interpret as the employee who has not appeared at work by the required time. By contrast, the man supplied by Brook Street is associated with being there 'on the dot'. But why is nine o'clock selected to represent this punctuality? Clearly, the advertisement would be counter-productive, if not meaningless, in a community where businesses began work at 7.00 a.m. or 8.00 a.m. or 8.30 a.m. Nor could Brook Street Bureau have been entirely happy with 9.00 a.m. as the focal point even in London — where some offices open earlier and many somewhat later, such as 9.30 a.m. or 10.00 a.m. But 9.00 a.m. was iconically the most satisfactory in forming an immediately recognisable geometric precision: the clock hands form an exact right-angle. And if nine o'clock is not the personal starting time for everyone reading the advertisement, at least it is familiar to all as a starting time for many.

Invisible man   Brook Street man

Fig. 4

On one final point the designers must also have felt some hesitation: the female version uses the term 'girl', the male 'man'. Doubtless, this is again a reasonable pragmatic compromise, though in most contexts *girl* matches *boy*, and *man* matches *woman*: and feminists are increasingly vocal in their objection to the use of 'girl' for a female employee because of its implied emphasis on youth, and hence a person over whom authority is wielded (cf Lecture Eight below). Yet for many outside that movement, *woman* sounds uneasily impolite and *lady* inappropriately suburban and class-oriented. It is of some interest that public lavatories in the USA (and elsewhere too in the English-speaking world) often bear the imbalanced labels 'Men' and 'Ladies'.

I have dwelt at length with the issues raised by some very ordinary, day-to-day examples to make the point that even the simplest, shortest, least technical, least momentous texts have a structure involving profound interactions between language and the world, between individuals and the culture in which they operate: involving extensive assumptions about shared knowledge and shared attitudes, reasoned inferences about the degree to which participants in even such simple communications are willing to co-operate. The desirable opposite of 'sloppy' is 'neat' or 'efficient': why should I, the reader, be willing to accept an otherwise unattested paraphrase of this as 'Brook Street'? Why indeed should I accept a neat vase of flowers as a promise of efficient typing? The opposite of 'invisible' (which would never occur to me as a word to apply to someone who was late for work) is 'visible'. But visibility is very low indeed in my priorities in seeking a useful colleague. Why should I equate visibility with punctuality — and this in turn with staff supplied by the Brook Street Bureau?

The answers to all these questions lie at the roots of human communication. We start with a disposition to *seek meaning*: to co-operate (cf Grice, 1975; Leech, 1983) in interpreting phenomena as in some way semiotic. But just as important: we are disposed to belief in the truth of the communciation and in its relevance. And its relevance entails being of value and interest to us as telling us something new and worthwhile. If our examples had been as in Fig. 5, they would of course have been easier to understand, in some ways more logical. But they would have been so simplistic, so obvious, so trite as to fail in arousing our interest or in conveying any sense of relevance. And they would have required additional indicators to connect the second part of each with the advertiser.

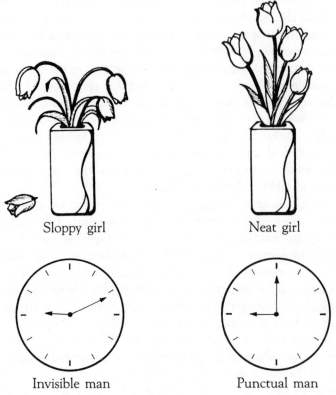

Fig. 5

Nonetheless, these simplified versions underlie the more interesting and more exacting ones that constituted the actual Brook
Street advertisements. They are what we need to see as the covert
intratextual constituents: 'sloppy' entails our awareness of an an-
tonym. But it must now be clear that the effectiveness of a text
depends not just on such intratextual constituents but on *extratextual* ones. Some of these are pictorial and cultural (as with the
vases of flowers), some may be *intertextual*. The latter make covert
or overt reference to another text of which shared knowledge can
be assumed: the use of the phrase 'invisible man' is of this kind,
connecting the text of the Brook Street advertisement to the title
and text of the Wells novel about a man who could move around
invisibly.

Let me illustrate these three distinctions — intratextual, extratextual, and intertextual — with examples that stay within language

without support from pictorial representation. Consider a text consisting of just the following two sentences:

> The trade minister has presented a persuasive case for stopping the export of strategically sensitive materials. Industry must look at this question very seriously indeed.

If the second sentence were to begin with the word *so*, the relation between the two sentences would be interpreted purely as *intratextual*. Because we now know the minister's policy, industry must obviously take the hint and consider what action is needed in consequence. But if the second sentence were to begin with the word *but*, the relation between the two sentences would have to be interpreted in terms of *extratextual* factors. Although it is clear which policy the minister is favouring, the writer would suggest by *but* that industry should take other factors into consideration and be very hesitant about accepting the policy. As linked by *so*, the reader need not look beyond the text in front of him; as linked by *but*, he is obliged to do so.

Now the other, but of course related, concept of *intertextual* reference. In Anita Brookner's recent prize-winning novel *Hotel du Lac*, the principal character is writing a letter about having been persuaded to take a holiday abroad: it had been thought that she was on the verge of a breakdown. Well, she says,

> I am myself now, and was then, although this fact was not recognised. Not drowning but waving.

The relation between these sentences is *intertextual*, our understanding being dependent upon our knowing the anecdote (subject of a well-known poem by Stevie Smith) of the seaside death which was caused by witnesses misinterpreting the thrashing arms of a man in the water: he died because people thought he was merely waving to friends on the shore when in fact he was drowning. Miss Brookner takes the key words from this totally different text and reverses them: her friends had thought she was metaphorically drowning when she was merely, so to say, waving.

That four-word sentence, 'Not drowning but waving', ends a paragraph which Miss Brookner began with another intertextual allusion:

> A cold coming I had of it. Penelope drove fast and kept her eyes grimly ahead ...

For anyone who does not recognise the modified quotation from
T.S. Eliot (the beginning of his *Journey of the Magi* just as it is
the beginning of the Brookner character's letter), the English will
seem curiously unidiomatic and its reference uncertain: is the writer
commenting on the weather or on the unfriendliness of her companion? Someone less confident about inferring the knowledge of
the reader might have felt driven to insert 'as Eliot almost said' at
this point in the letter, and to add at the other point: 'if I may
invert the circumstances of the man whose friends let him die'.
Redundancy is valuable — often indeed essential — in communication, but there are severe penalties for over-indulgence.

Virtually every communication depends on supplementing
the lexical and grammatical coherence achieved intratextually by
pronominalisation, paraphrase, and other purely linguistic devices.
We have to refer outward to other texts and outward beyond
other texts to features of the world around us.[1] This is relatively
easy in spoken discourse within our own circle of acquaintances
but becomes more difficult as we write — and especially as we
write for audiences unknown and beyond the confines of our own
familiar culture. At this moment, there are hurtling towards the
stars several space-craft, the Pioneers and Voyagers, which have on
board information that we seek to convey to possible dwellers in
other worlds: a mixture of electronic, pictorial, and mathematical
devices is accompanied by recorded excerpts in many human languages. It is hoped that other civilisations will want to interpret
these communications and will co-operate in seeking to do so.
But this is an extreme example of where nothing beyond this
co-operative maxim can be taken for granted. We can assume no
shared knowledge at all, and it is impossible to be confident in
attempting discourse in these circumstances.

The point I wish to make as my last in this first lecture is that,
because English is so widely used in the world for communicating
between peoples of different linguistic and cultural backgrounds,
we should never forget the gaps it may be necessary to bridge
as we make our intertextual and extratextual allusions. In 1982,

---

[1]There is an especially remarkable degree of intertextuality in slogans and
advertising. A series in sausage promotion included 'I'm meaty — fry me' (echoing the air hostess in another advertising series, 'I'm Susan — fly me'), 'Porky and
best' (echoing 'Porgy and Bess'), among others. The musicians' charity *Bandaid*
carries an appropriate reference to a proprietary brand of emergency plaster,
which itself — with equal appropriacy — invites identification with 'first aid'.

there was an international educational conference in Dubrovnik, Jugoslavia. One of the participants was a friend of mine, Professor Ramesh Mohan, then head of the Indian Central Institute in Hyderabad, and he sent me a copy of the paper he had circulated, presenting very important numerical data about the expansion of higher education in India. It is of some interest in the present connection to consider one excerpt from Mohan's paper:

> Correspondence courses ... are already being conducted by 22 universities, with an enrolment of 1,15,000.

Let us leave aside for a moment how this would sound if the last figure were given orally. As written, it constitutes a puzzle for anyone outside the Indian subcontinent and other areas using Indian numerology. Elsewhere, if commas are used in long figures, they separate units of three digits counting from the right. In such cultures, Mohan's figure looks like a misprint: is the first comma to be deleted or is there a digit missing between the two commas? The fact is, of course, that there is no error: the method of punctuating the digits reflects precisely the Indian mode of referring to units larger than a thousand. The quantity that the rest of us refer to analytically as 'a hundred thousand' is for Indians lexicalised as a *lakh*, a hundred of which in turn is lexicalised as a *crore*. Mohan's secretary therefore correctly represented in figures the total of 1.15 *lakhs* of students doing university correspondence courses. In India, Mohan would probably have given the total orally as 'more than one *lakh*'; in the international setting of the Dubrovnik conference, he probably verbalised this same quantity as 'more than a hundred thousand'.

The point for our purposes is simply this: every communication in every language is impregnated with culture-bound references. As we move from using language in the environments with which we are most familiar, we are faced with the need to recognise what those culture-determined features and allusions are. Will our readers be familiar enough with tennis to understand the phrase 'in straight sets'? Will they associate angular letters with Greece? Will they know that there has been work on a new range-finder? Will they know, indeed, what a range-finder is? Have they ever heard of *The Invisible Man*? Will they associate nine o'clock with starting work? Have they read T.S. Eliot's *Journey of the Magi*? If we think that all these things are beyond our readers' comprehension, we are in danger of reducing our communication to banality, sacrificing the fun of puzzling it out, losing our readers' interest: 'The employee you hire from others will always be late for work: you can depend on our man to be on time.' If on the other hand we wrongly assume that *lakhs* and *crores* and H.G. Wells and range-finders and T.S. Eliot and Brook Street Bureau are totally familiar to our readers, we are in the opposite danger of leaving them totally at sea. Not waving but drowning.

Lecture Two
Strategies of Beginning

We communicate in *texts* (cf Quirk *et al.*, 1985): that is, in stretches of language — spoken or written, short or long — which effect the semiotic and pragmatic correlation which we discussed in my first lecture. And in that lecture, I stressed the importance, as well as the inherent difficulty, of trying to establish and then keep firmly in mind the shared knowledge of communicator and addressee. We are able to make a communication effective only by saying something new. But that 'something new' has to be linked to 'something old': we have to start from where the addressee is now (cf Chafe, 1976). I used an allusion to T.S. Eliot in connection with the shared-knowledge precept. Let me use Eliot again in connection with the theme I want to address now. In his *Four Quartets* he reminds us that in communication 'every attempt Is a wholly new start', 'each venture Is a new beginning, a raid on the inarticulate'. I shall get away from the military metaphor on which he embarks and direct your attention to the anatomical one implied by 'inarticulate'.

In its formative stages, the communication we wish to make is like a number of bones, laying around in the newly dug archaeological site of our minds, each bone unjoined to any other: unordered, inarticulate. The completed communication will have each bone placed in purposive relation to another, sets of such bones constituting one unit, such as an arm or a leg, which then as a whole is purposively articulated to a shoulder or a pelvis. Once we have started, it will not be so bad: but where do we begin?

To carry this macabre analogy a little further, we are more in the position of having a collection of bones that must be articulated with another — and, we trust, a complementary — collection in the possession of our addressee. How do we select a bone in our collection that will obviously link up with one in his? Well, of course, one way is to ask him what bones he has in his collection and then promptly set to work fitting an appropriate one from ours.

25

So it is that, in opening up a conversation with someone, we often begin with a question, and this can have more than one function: exploring our hearer's existing knowledge, invoking participation and interest, and thirdly indicating the topic on which we hope to convey some new information:

> Have you been anywhere near Soho this afternoon?
> Well, there's a huge fire and several buildings are gutted.
> It seems to have started with a gas explosion in a kitchen
> but by now several streets have been sealed off and West
> End traffic is in absolute chaos.

I have tried to illustrate this interrogative gambit with something that might be heard between two acquaintances meeting in the street or equally between total strangers in a shop or a train. But in fact, apart from when we are embarking on discussions of severe emergencies, discourse beginnings tend to be very different as between family and friends on the one hand and strangers on the other. It is with the former that we go straight to the point — and often, as I say, with a question. And if 'existing knowledge' is less important because we know more about our addressee in this respect, it remains just as important to invoke the other's participation and give some indication of what is to follow:

> Do you know who came in to the office this afternoon?
> Do you hear that confounded dog again?

Whether, as in the first of these, the answer could hardly be other than 'No' or, as in the second, it could hardly be other than 'Yes', such questions are not meant to elicit answers, but interested attention. As such, they can be reduced to the merest 'phatic communion' with a question that is interrogative in form only:

> Do you know what? I think it's time I wrote a will. I'll
> ask Jack if he can recommend a good lawyer.

And since no one who asks 'Have you heard the one about the teacher's daughter?' expects the addressee to say 'Yes', this opening can be taken as a phatic gesture that the speaker wants to tell a joke. But of course question openings are by no means confined to indicating the will to convey information or tell jokes. They can also be used — obviously — to seek it. The strategy is none the less identical. The opening speaker defines by his question the direction that the conversation should take. In the case of the 'fire' example, the questioner might well have paused after

> Have you been anywhere near Soho this afternoon?

And if there is an affirmative response, the questioner might at once come back with

> Well, please tell me more. I gather there's a huge fire ...

Moreover, information-*seeking* questions may be as phatic as the information-*offering* question 'Do you know what?' For example, one may informally invite news, information, grumbles, comment, with such openers as

> How goes it?
> How's things?
> What's new?

For the purposes of the present lecture, of course, I am not concerned with how we break the conversational ice among family and friends. We all manage these things pretty well without academic lectures on the subject. I mention this type of situation precisely because it *is* familiar and therefore constitutes our only experience of 'how to start' when we are faced with the prospect of starting something less familiar: like beginning a talk on the radio, or composing an article for a newspaper, or even writing an academic lecture.

The familiar openings we have been considering have two vital features that we must carry over into these less familiar settings. We need to evoke the participatory attention of our listeners or readers. And we need to give them some idea of why we want it. Not surprisingly, we find ourselves adapting such strategies as the question, partly because they come naturally to us, and partly because we can infer that our hearers or readers will be used to such gambits as well. A letter to the press might thus begin as follows:

> How many of your readers are aware of the connection between car radios and traffic accidents? Studying police reports of some fifteen accidents this year, I have found that in twelve of them, the drivers were listening to radios at the time of impact, and it seems very likely that in consequence their attention was to some

extent deflected from the necessary concentration on
their driving.

Even in a situation where help and information are going to be
provided by a particular participant, it is quite likely that this very
participant will open the discourse, and that with a question (often
preceded by *well*: cf Lecture Five). A doctor in his surgery may greet
the next patient with:

Well now, Mrs Jones, what seems to be the problem?

A teacher may begin a lesson with:

Well, shall we begin where we left off last week? Do
you remember the distinction I drew between speed
and acceleration?

Meeting a new class, a teacher may instinctively seek to interest
and involve pupils with a question such as:

Well, now, how about getting to know each other?

And of course directives and requests are often dressed up as questions — if only for courtesy's sake:

Will you tell me your name, please?

Would you care to come in now, Mrs Jones?

Could you set quietly and let me explain?

And questions must be taken to include *indirect* questions:

I wonder whether you would care to give me your name.

My concern is how to apply for a renewal of this licence.

Nor should we forget the question-related structure called the
'pseudo-cleft' (Quirk *et al.*, 1985):

What I would like to do this afternoon is explore with
you the strategies of discoursal openings.

I do not mean to give the impression, of course, that all
discourse begins in an interrogative mode. Within the circle of
intimates, we can open up with an imperative:

Just listen to this, folks!

(so, too, within living memory, but well beyond the circle of intimates, the town-crier's 'Oyez! Oyez! Oyez!') or

> Switch the radio off a minute and let me tell you about
> a problem that's cropped up.

We may also begin with an exclamation:

> What a ghastly day! I've been drenched coming here.
>
> How marvellous about Betty! You must be very proud
> of her success.

More formally, an alternative opening can make use of a polite
conditional:

> If I may, I'd be grateful for your attention so that I
> can explain ...
>
> If you could spare a moment, perhaps you could tell
> me ...
>
> If everyone is ready, perhaps we can begin the meeting.

Of course, there are situations in which conventions of a different
kind are accepted:

> Your attention please. Singapore Airlines announce the
> departure of Flight SQ 58 for Hong Kong.
>
> BBC Radio 4. The time is now two o'clock and here
> is a summary of the news.
>
> This is an answering machine. When you hear the bleep,
> please give your name and phone number, together with
> a short message, and we shall call you back as soon
> as possible.

It is worth noticing that, with the last, a still rather unfamiliar mode
of communication, it is usual — as in this example — to suggest
to callers how they should structure their message: in other words,
we *tell* them how to begin.

It may seem strange that by this time I still have not mentioned
other familiar formulae for beginnings — formulae sanctified by
tradition to a far greater extent than obtains with radio or public
address systems. For example, in many — perhaps all — cultures,
there is a well-established and immediately recognisable way of

beginning a story. Chinese tales often begin by naming a person:

> There was a certain young man named Yu who was fond of boxing ...
>
> There was a native of Shun Tian named Xing Yunfei, who was a lover of stones ...
>
> There lived in Ling Yang a man named Zhu Erdan ...
>
> Ma Ji, whose alternative name was Longmei, was the son of a merchant ...
>
> A certain Xu, a native of Jiaozhou, was engaged in trade beyond the sea ...
>
> In Taiyuan there was a certain gentleman named Geng who came of an old and well-known family ...[1]

On the other side of the world, the sagas of medieval Iceland began likewise and indeed with far less variance:

> Thorstein was the name of a man; he was the son of Egil Skallagrimsson ...
>
> Mord was the name of a man; he also had the name of Fiddle and he was the son of Sigvat the Red ...[2]

Well, of course, the English language provides similar formulae. The very first of Chaucer's Canterbury Tales begins:

> Whilom, as olde stories tellen us,
> Ther was a duc that highte Theseus.

The formula survives in stories for children whose young hearts are stirred as a fond parent begins: 'Once upon a time, there was a poor woodman who lived in the Forest of Dean ...'

I had not mentioned these conventions, because they are very much associated with fiction and — so far as the Anglo-Saxon tradition is concerned at any rate — with fiction of bygone days. And they are fictional not least in purporting to represent something that has a real beginning: we affect to start with a *tabula rasa* in which everything is postulated as new. In the non-fictional world, as I have tried to show elsewhere (Quirk, 1982, Chapter 11),

---

[1] All these examples are taken from the translations in *Strange Tales of Liaozhai*. (Hong Kong: Commercial Press, 1982).

[2] The openings of *Gunnlaugssaga* and *Njalssaga* respectively (my own translation).

'beginnings do not exist: we have only continuations'. To the extent that the examples given earlier in this lecture have seemed plausible, this statement may strike you as blatantly flying in the face of the facts.

Not so. I invite your attention to discourse as 'continuation' — and this in two fairly distinct respects: what we may think of as the escalator model and the elevator model. Spoken discourse in which we participate is usually already in progress when we join it. Rather than pressing a button to start an elevator moving, we are more usually involved in getting on to an escalator which already has passengers and which is already in motion. We join a group of acquaintances, trying not to be so intrusive as to stop their conversation, and we listen for a few moments, tune in to the topic as best we can, and in due course make a contribution of our own, not to introduce a new subject but to add our own continuation to the one already in progress.

It is with this fact that the modern realistic novel comes to terms, no longer opening with a traditional and formulaic beginning such as the ones we have just been exemplifying. Patrick White's novel *The Twyborn Affair* (1979) begins as follows:

> 'Which road this afternoon, Madam?'
> 'The same, Teakle — the one we took yesterday.'
> 'Bit rough, isn't it?' her chauffeur ventured.
> 'We Australians', Mrs Golson declared, 'are used to far rougher at home.'

It is just as though we had chanced to hear two strangers talking, and we eavesdrop our way into their lives. We speedily learn that it is a driver and his female employer: we speedily learn that the latter is an Australian called Mrs Golson, and that wherever she is, she is not at the moment of speaking in Australia itself.

I referred to this technique as that of 'the modern realistic novel', but of course it is not all that modern — nor has it been confined to the novel. For hundreds of years, we have been used to such openings in drama. For example, Shakespeare's *Taming of the Shrew* begins with a man and a woman on stage, as much strangers to us as were Patrick White's chauffeur and employer. The man speaks first:

> I'll pheeze you,[1] in faith.

---

[1] A vague threat.

And the woman replies:

> A pair of stocks, you rogue!

to which the man responds with:

> Y'are a baggage: the Slys are no rogues; look in the
> chronicles: we came in with Richard Conqueror.

As with the Patrick White example, our eavesdropping quickly yields results: we learn the man's name (it is Sly) and we know that he has social pretensions far above the level of the woman with whom he is in conflict.

This literary convention implicitly asserts that whatever may constitute the sense of ending, conclusion, finality to which the novel or play is directed, there is no beginning: only a plunging into activities and relationships that are already there. We join in a process which is *continuing*.

So much for the 'escalator', the first respect in which I suggested we might regard discourse as continuation. For the second, the 'elevator' model, let us return to my insistence in the first lecture upon shared knowledge. We noted the extreme and limiting case of the unmanned space-craft equipped with an attempt to begin discourse with the inhabitants of possible worlds, light-years away in the galaxy, creatures of whose existence we know nothing, and in breaking silence with whom we can make no assumptions of shared knowledge whatsoever. In communicating with our fellow human beings on earth, we are in a totally different position: we know that there is and must be shared knowledge, and we know that in any new communication we must build a bridge from that common basis, providing an extension, a continuation that is as smooth as our tact and ingenuity can make it.

Even a newspaper article (or news broadcast) about a totally unforeseen happening is likely to be linked back to a known analogy. Thus, announcing the volcanic devastation in Colombia in the autumn of 1985, news items appeared like the following:

> Only weeks after the disaster in Mexico, a possibly even
> greater one has befallen her neighbour Colombia, a few
> hundred miles to the south-east. Many thousands of
> people are feared to have lost their lives when Nevado
> del Ruiz gave vent to a massive volcanic eruption.

We notice that the actual news is given only in the second of these two sentences, and if economy and speed were our only criteria, the first sentence might have been omitted altogether. Yet in discourse strategy the first sentence is essential, forming as it does the bridge that continues past experience on to new experience. A continuation in more relevant senses than one. Disasters are unhappily the continuing lot of mankind. There is more immediately the continuation of recent experience: the Mexico tragedy, still fresh in all our minds. There is the consequent continuity to recently endorsed geographical knowledge: Mexico, still unhappily associated with such news, is used topographically as the link to Colombia, whose exact location could not otherwise be taken as common knowledge for Europeans. Even fewer would know where Nevado del Ruiz was, nor that it was a mountain, still less a volcanic one. There will even be, for some readers, an implication of geological continuity: the two Latin-American events may not be seismological coincidences.

So much for what we might call the *pragmatics* of continuation in this example. Now let us look at the language that conveys this connectivity.

Linguistic means of indicating to addressees that we are continuing on from what they already know include that very lightly stressed item, the definite article. To begin an observation as follows:

The range-finder has been destroyed …

not merely indicates that the addressees are assumed to know what *a* range-finder is, but that they know well *which* range-finder the sentence refers to. So in our example, the opening words include the noun phrase *the disaster in Mexico*: '*the* disaster' that you and I know about is our shared point of departure; we can now continue with something to which your previous knowledge and experience are relevant. It is both grammatically and communicatively appropriate, therefore, that the noun phrase we have been considering is immediately followed by another that is clearly related: so immediate and so clearly related that the connection can be pointed by suppressing the common element *disaster* and replacing it by the pronoun *one*: 'a possibly even greater *one*'. But there is a further grammatical difference between the two neighbouring noun phrases; the definite article has been replaced by the indefinite: '*a* possibly even greater one'. Start from our shared knowledge of *the* disaster you know about and I will tell you about *a* disaster that you don't.

If we now recall the examples of textual beginnings that we have been considering in this lecture, the prominent role of this most unprominent indefinite article will be appreciated: 'a huge fire' in Soho; time to write 'a will' and see 'a good lawyer'; and in translation from both Chinese and Icelandic, 'a certain young man', 'a native of Jiaozhou', 'Thorstein was the name of a man'.

All these indefinite noun phrases have a further grammatical feature in common which is highly relevant to the strategies of beginning a discourse. This feature can be seen with special clarity if the first sentence of the eruption report is re-written, preserving exactly the information content of the original but changing the sequence of presentation:

> A possibly even greater disaster has befallen Colombia
> only weeks after the one in Mexico, her neighbour a
> few hundred miles to the north-west.

We observe that there is nothing ungrammatical about this version, yet considered as the initiating sentence of a news item, it is decidedly odd. True, the new disaster is correctly prefixed by the indefinite signal and the familiar one by the definite. But the order in this alternative version not merely entails defining the location of the familiar disaster in relation to the previously unknown one, but of requiring the reader to *begin* by registering a new event and of only *subsequently* being enabled to relate this to previous knowledge. In other words, the alternative presentation frustrates the 'continuation' principle of proceeding from the shared 'known' to the communicated 'new'. This directionality, so obvious in pedagogy and logic alike, has a linguistic icon in *linearity*: we order the lexical and grammatical constituents of a communication, bearing in mind the desirability of a real-time presentation in which the familiar precedes the unfamiliar.

In linguistic studies, especially as conducted by the Prague School, this is known as achieving 'functional sentence perspective' (FSP), and we shall be considering its implications in more detail later (especially in the fifth lecture). But there is one feature of FSP that we should discuss at this point: it is the notion of *topic*. We apply this term to the grammatical unit which is initially placed in the sentence and, given the correspondence of linguistic linearity with logical progression — as we have seen — from most familiar to least familiar, it follows that the 'topic' has special reference to the 'most familiar' end of this scale. In many and perhaps the most

typical English sentences, the 'topic' is isomorphous with the grammatical 'subject'. Both terms are used in an obviously non-accidental
correspondence with their ordinary meanings: first we must know
the topic or subject under discussion, then we can go on and learn
something about it. For example:

> My car needs an oil-change.

Here, as simultaneously subject and topic, *my car* shows that it is
to be expected that the addressee knows I have a car[1]: we can now
continue on from that shared knowledge to say something relevant
but — so far as the addressee is concerned — presumed to be new.
(In fact it may not be new and the addressee may reply 'Yes, I know:
your husband told me': the fact that one doesn't expect to have
to make such replies is confirmation of the point I am making.)
Let us suppose that the reply is:

> An oil-change my poor old car has needed for weeks,
> but I never seem to find time.

Here the topic is not the grammatical subject but the object of the
sentence, though we see at once that its choice as topic is as well
motivated as was *my car* in the sentence to which this is a response.
The issue of oil-change, having been raised by the first speaker, is
now the relevant common ground between the participants and
is thus appropriately used as the topical base for a further continuation of the communicative process.

We may now look back at the original disaster report in the
light of this discussion. It began as follow:

> Only weeks after the disaster in Mexico, a possibly even
> greater one has befallen her neighbour Colombia ...

Again the topic is not the subject of the sentence: this time it is
the *adverbial* element as realised by the rather long phrase, *only
weeks after the disaster in Mexico*. The Mexican disaster is thus
signalled as shared knowledge both by the definite article as discussed earlier and by the topicalisation of the phrase in which it
occurs (together with another reminder of shared knowledge: the
fact that it took place only recently). It is worth noting too that

---

[1]Or that it is a cultural norm; a similar noun phrase as topic may indeed be a
universal, with the 'shared knowledge' therefore inherent: e.g. 'My back is aching'.

the use of such signals as definiteness and topicalisation work both ways: they reflect the speaker's assumption that these things are likely to be familiar to the addressee, but they function equally as the speaker's suggestion that they *ought* to be. They tell the addressee that what follows is based on the premise that particular items of knowledge are being taken for granted. Where necessary, therefore, having received this warning, the less well-informed reader may turn to a companion and ask some such question as 'What's this Mexican disaster that we seem to be expected to know about?'

We have now sufficiently explored the role of topicalisation and definiteness in indicating a starting point in jointly-held knowledge and in providing the proper sense of all communication being a continuation from known to less known data. It may be objected that plenty of discourse-initiating sentences, even between strangers, have a definite topic with no such warranty. True. We can instance the plausible remark (in societies where silence can be broken with phatic meteorological comment) by a stranger in a bus queue:

The weather's turning nasty.

And we can contrast an implausible utterance in the same circumstances and with the same apparent grammar:

The chairman's turning nasty.

Confronted by this second remark, one may be startled into saying 'What chairman?' or 'Sorry, were you speaking to me?' — both questions prompted by the knowledge that such an utterance could be expected to pass only between acquaintances for whom *the chairman* had been independently identified. But on being addressed by the superficially similar

The weather's turning nasty

no one is going to look startled and ask 'What weather?' This is because, although the two sentences are indeed similar in form (the topic is the subject and the subject is a definite noun phrase in both), the uses of the definite article are sharply different. In *the chairman*, we interpret *the* as anaphoric since the noun concerned is one that can have an indefinite number of quite discrete referents. We therefore require definiteness to arise from some such sequence — in language or experience — as the following:

> Have you appointed *a chairman* yet, and if so what is
> *the chairman*'s name?

With *the weather*, the relations of noun and article are quite different, and the identity of the referent is provided by a society's general knowledge. Since it is not·possible to ask

> Is there *any weather* this morning, and if so, what is
> *the weather* like?

we see that the definite article with this noun is not anaphoric. We further see not merely why it is perfectly possible to begin discourses with a stranger by saying

> The weather's turning nasty

but also the sense in which this example does not frustrate the rule that all communication is a continuation. The weather is grammatically marked as constituting precisely the kind of shared knowledge from which continuation is natural.[1]

But there may be further objection to this theory of communication. Even accepting that definite phrases are normally in some sense continuations from earlier experience, how can the first *indefinite* noun phrase connect backwards if by definition it is new information? For example:

> (1) Excuse me, can you help me find a little boy in a
> blue shirt?

> (2) Excuse me, can you help me find a doctor?

To explicate the way in which both these are rational continuations from or projections of shared experience, we need to pause and examine the meaning of the indefinite article. In the likeliest interpretation of (1), the article with *boy* and *shirt* is used somewhat

---

[1]As with the earlier example of *my car*, a fuller discussion would reveal many additional points. 'I saw it in the paper' uses a definite article which does not depend on previous reference but on the expectations determined by cultural norms. In 'The reason I've asked you to come is this', the definite article is again not anaphoric; in this instance, it is cataphoric, referring the addressee *forward* in the discourse. Something similar accounts for the definite article in titles such as *The Tempest* or *The Cocktail Party*. Moreover, in such discourse as advertising or in media announcements, a definite article can arouse interest by so to say 'pretending' to be anaphoric.

in the way we found it in connection with the Colombian disaster: it indicates specific reference and the speaker might have added 'I've looked everywhere for *him*'. But whereas with the Colombian disaster the continuation feature was contextually determined by the earlier (i.e. intratextual) mention of the Mexican disaster, continuation here relates to general (i.e. extratextual) experience. Can you help me find a certain one of those human beings that we can all be expected to recognise as a young male child, dressed in one of those garments which it is again plausible to assume you would recognise as a blue shirt? In other words, we ask the addressee to go on from what we take to be common ground in our experience of the world and in our linguistic conventions of naming it.

In (2), the position is rather different. Here, again in the likeliest interpretation, the indefinite article indicates that the noun has a descriptive role rather than a referring one. There is then no question of the speaker having in mind a specific medical practitioner who could be named (say 'Margaret Turner'), as the little boy in (1) could be named. And in contrast to (1), an addition would more likely have been 'I've looked everywhere for *one*'. The question could therefore be laboriously paraphrased as 'Can you help me find any particular one of those persons qualified in medicine such as are in common parlance described as doctors?' Otherwise, the *point du depart* of both questions is similarly based on an assumed extratextual shared experience from which we may safely proceed.

There is however a basis in pragmatics for regarding (1) and (2) as continuations, and here again there is a clear difference between (1) and (2) which is dependent on the role of the indefinite article as well as on the lexical meaning of the two head nouns, *boy* and *doctor*. With (1), the addressee recognises a familiar context: a lost child and a consequently anxious parent. With (2), the addressee recognises a covert announcement of a different type of emergency: the speaker is urgently seeking someone who can give medical help.

One important way in which beginnings can introduce indefinite noun phrases which, like those in (1) and (2), take us into assumed shared experience without contextual preparation is the *existential* sentence, as in

> There's a big fire in Soho.
>
> Is there a doctor around?
>
> There's a little boy missing.

In thus beginning with a topic which is abstract, non-referential, and context-free, we signal to the addressee that the 'new' element (the indefinite noun phrase) must be related to our knowledge of the language and our world before further development of the communication is possible. When we were earlier considering traditional formulae for beginning a discourse, we encountered just such existential openings, though without naming them as such:

> There was a certain young man named Yu ...
>
> Ther was a duc that highte Theseus ...

We now see perhaps that both (1) and (2) resemble the existential device in using such topics and sentence structures as may leave it clear that the purpose is only to focus attention upon the uncontextualised indefinite noun phrase with which the questions end.

Such variants of the existential *there* plus *be* formula are widely used for beginnings, whether beginnings of entirely new discourses or beginnings of new sections within a discourse:

> Here is an important announcement ...
>
> I have a friend I'd like to introduce to you ...
>
> We come now to a new problem ...
>
> Can I invite your attention to an exhibition that is opening at the Courtauld next week?

We are at last in a position to look more critically at the rather pessimistic pronouncement by T.S. Eliot with which I began this lecture. Whatever difficulties we are going to encounter in finding and ordering and structuring the appropriate words to express ourselves in the body of a discourse, it is not the case that in beginning it we are embarking with a *tabula rasa*, involving a totally 'new beginning', 'a wholly new start'. We are either starting off from shared knowledge to which we make explicit reference (as with the Mexican disaster) or from knowledge which we can be so confident is shared that we can assume it implicitly ('I need a doctor'). We are not so much beginning as continuing.

We begin such continuing, moreover, in the comfortable knowledge that our addressee wishes to be addressed, wishes to become interested, wishes to co-operate in the discourse on which we are embarking. Indeed, however politely and diffidently we excuse our intrusion or question our way into our addressee's attention,

our confidence in making an announcement about a plane's departure, beginning a lecture, composing a news story for the front page,
or even writing the first paragraph of a learned monograph, needs
no reassurance. Our addressees have put themselves in the position of expecting, welcoming, even demanding the communication
we are making.

Moreover, discourse does not usually take place in a language-
sealed vacuum. It tends to be accompanied by a physical or at
any rate, a visual co-text. A motorway sign saying 'No U-Turns' does
not need to be embedded in an existential sentence such as 'There
must be no U-Turns here' because you are already 'here'
driving on the motorway when you read it. Somewhat analogously,
where serious commitment can be assumed in the addressee, discourse can open with uncompromising directness. A book by John
Bowle published in 1979 (London: Secker and Warburg) has as its
first sentence:

> Africa, not Europe or even Eurasia, is now thought to
> have been the original habitat of mankind.

Few concessions here, you may think, to the strategies of agreeing
shared knowledge such as have preoccupied us in this lecture. But
of course, although it is the first actual sentence, it has been preceded
by a chapter heading, 'The Palaeolithic Hunters'; and (ignoring the
equally precedent Introduction and Preface) we note that this heading took its place in a still earlier list of Contents from which
a reader can see the relation between that first chapter and the
further forty-odd which follow. More relevant still, all this is preceded
by a title page which, like the cover, proclaims that the book —
this total discourse — is *A History of Europe: A Cultural and Political Survey*. Here, you may say, is the real beginning; this is the
existential opening — just as if we heard the author saying 'Here
is a history of Europe'. No wonder that Bowle feels able to plunge
into his first page with the uncompromising initial sentence just
quoted. He knows that he can assume the common starting point,
and the ready co-operative interest that goes with it, from the very
fact that any reader must have bought the book or selected it from
the shelves of the library.

So let us have done with the pains, problems, and strategies
of breaking forth from silence. We can now turn to the body of
the discourse itself and consider the part played within it of locational and temporal reference.

Lecture Three
Location and the Creation of a World

Let us look again for a moment at some of the text beginnings that we considered in the previous lecture:

> There lived in Lingyang a man named Zhu Erdan ...
>
> In Taiyuan there was a certain gentleman named Geng ...
>
> Only weeks after the disaster in Mexico ...
>
> There's a big fire in Soho.
>
> Is there a doctor around?

It is to be noted that each contains a formal reference to physical location. Whether made the topic as thematic background (for example, with *In Taiyuan...*), or represented as the final and focal part of the opening sentence (for example, with the 'rhematic' *in Soho*), a local or geographical setting seems to be required, in terms of which the communication is to be understood and the addressee given firm orientation. Doubtless true of human language generally (two of the above examples are translated from Chinese), it is dramatically true of English, in which it is typically expressed through the *adverbial* element in sentence structure.

Extrapolating from a large sample of spoken and written discourse in the Survey of English Usage, we can say that there is an adverbial in every seven or eight words of running text (Quirk *et al.*, 1985, p. 489). To take prepositional phrases alone (the biggest class of realisation types as well as the class that arguably refers most precisely), more relate to *location* — some 28 per cent — than to any other adverbial meaning. This is strikingly impressive when we consider the wide range of semantic relations expressed by adverbials as a whole: approximation (for example, *almost*), restriction (*only*), amplification (*increasingly*), diminution (*a little*), measure (*very much*), cause (*from cancer*), reason (*because of her illness*), purpose (*to study English*), result, condition, concession, respect, manner, means, instrument, agency (as in 'She was treated *by a doctor*'), frequency, span (as in *for two weeks*); all these in addition to the relationships to do with location. Yet it is with this last-mentioned category that more than a quarter of all adverbial prepositional phrases are concerned.

Let us therefore look more closely at the role of locatives in discourse. The five illustrations with which I began all concern initial scene-setting: they indicate the location with reference to which the discourse will take place (even the short adverbial *around* in the fifth example means 'in the immediate vicinity of the speaker and addressee'). But if localisers were used only to set the scene, they would not occur as frequently as they do in every text. They are a continuous recourse for supplying connections (with respect to that point of reference) throughout the discourse. You will recall the example about the horrifying events in Colombia:

> Only weeks after the disaster *in Mexico*, a possibly even greater one has befallen her nieghbour Colombia, a few hundred miles *to the south-east*.

Not only does this last phrase relate elliptically to the earlier location reference ('to the south-east *of Mexico*'), it relocates the new focus of the narrative for the addressee in relation to this original orientation marker. It is thus useful to see location markers as *absolute* or *relative*, provided we recognise that absolute is itself relative. I may say, for instance, that I own a villa exactly fifteen degrees longitude east and forty-seven degrees latitude north. This is about as absolute as one can be. Alternatively, I may say that the villa is near Graz. This is partly absolute, partly relative, and it has a better chance of being understood in relation to my addressee's knowledge and experience. It would have a better chance still if it were more explicitly relative: my villa is a hundred kilometres or so south-west of Vienna, the capital of Austria.

Let us consider a longer example, composed as a witness's report to the police; the adverbial locatives are italicised:

> I was *at the front door* talking to a caller. Suddenly, we heard a crash *nearby*, looked *round us*, and *there* we saw *in the street*, but *just a few houses beyond mine*, two cars that had obviously collided. We hurried *along to the spot* to see if we could help. One driver was scrambling *out* with blood on his face, and my companion helped him

> *over to the pavement.* By then some other people were
> running *up the street* and I dashed *back in* to phone
> the emergency services. When I came *out* again, people
> called me *over* to help move one of the cars *down the*
> *road* a little and *in to the side* because by this time there
> were other cars *from both directions* trying to get *past.*

The basic location is given, appropriately, as the speaker's own
orientation point: 'at the front door'; that is, elliptically, the (main)
entrance of his home. All other locatives serve both to link the
parts of the report into a coherent whole and to relate them directly
or indirectly to this original location. The crash was *nearby, in the*
street where the speaker lived but *a few houses beyond* his own. After
going *to the spot* where the crash occured, the speaker dashed *back*
to where he lived and went *in* to telephone, then came *out* of his
home again and was called *over* to the crashed cars. So much for
the items having direct relation to the original point of orientation.

But in the course of the narrative a second orientation point
becomes established: the spot where the crash occured. After its
position has been related to the speaker's home, it becomes the
point to which other spatial references are then related. One driver
was helped *over to the pavement* — from the crash position; people
came running *up the street* — towards the crash; it was decided to
move one of the cars *down the road* — away from where it had
crashed, so that other vehicles could get *past* the crash position.
Finally, within this crash position, one of the vehicles involved
becomes an orientation point: 'One driver was scrambling *out*'.

But obviously salient as adverbials are in plotting location
and keeping an addressee fully oriented, the task is by no means
left to adverbials alone. Compare:

> The streets are kept exceptionally clean in Singapore.
>
> Singapore's streets are kept exceptionally clean.
>
> Singaporeans keep their streets exceptionally clean.

In all three, location is essential to the meaning, but it is expressed
in three different grammatical ways, only one of these ways involving an adverbial.

Moreover, this is to speak only of specific or absolute location.
But, as became clear in discussing the car crash, we are often far
more concerned with *relative* location: and especially with locative
orientation with respect to the speaker and the addressee. It is thus

that *perspective* is supplied, and this as we shall see is all important. The orientation can be expressed by verbs, and with some verbs orientation is alienable. Compare:

(1) When did you come?

(2) When did you go?

Question (1) entails that the addressee moved to a position that is regarded as near from the speaker's viewpoint; (2) entails that the addressee moved to a position regarded by the speaker as not near: it would be anomalous to extend it as 'When did you go here to my house?' Note equally:

> Are you coming with me or are you going with some-
> one else?

Indeed, relative locational orientation seems to be a more likely need felt in discourse than absolute orientation. True, the absolute location ('in Mexico') seems to be a very general interest — though its predominance in narrative may owe much to mere narrative convention: like the preoccupation with age in certain types of popular reportage ('A thirty-three year old employee at the Ministry of Defence was yesterday accused ...'). By contrast, orientation in respect of the addressee's world seems to be a requirement that goes far beyond the gossip value of interest or the whim of reportage style. At its most literal, it may be a reflex of biological 'territoriality' (cf again *come* and *go*). An insightful, if fictive, demonstration occurs in the Booker-prize novel *Hotel du Lac* to which I referred in my first lecture. Miss Brookner's heroine has newly arrived at the Swiss hotel, and she at once embarks on the letter to her lover back in London from which I have already quoted. She explains how talking to a fellow passenger on the plane had made the journey pass quickly, so that

> Within an extraordinarily short time we were there (I
> notice that I say 'there' and not 'here') and he put me
> in a taxi, and after about half an hour I ended up here
> (and it is beginning to be 'here' rather than 'there') ...

At first, *there* can still refer to the Swiss hotel though she has already arrived; her point of orientation is still London, her home and also that of the man with whom — significantly — she is mentally united through the act of letter-writing at the moment when she notices the illogicality induced by jet-lag (and emotion-lag). Almost simultaneously, she becomes aware of the new orientation (the hotel becomes 'here') and this is matched by the physical and (soon) the emotional distance from her lover.

The importance of local orientation is brought out strongly in an experiment reported by de Beaugrande (1980). Student subjects were briefly presented with a dozen-line text concerning a rocket blast-off and were then asked to write it down from memory as best they could. The fact that the text was presented in five different versions does not concern us in the present context. What does, however, is that among the differences between the original and the subjects' reconstructed versions were numerous additions, by far 'the most popular' being indicators of location. This interestingly confirms the role of locatives in the London Survey data (though here we drew only on locatives expressed by adverbials). But when we look at the particular locatives supplied by de Beaugrande's students, we find that for the most part they are not *absolute* but *relative* localisers: markers of orientation to the perceived author or observer, in fact. Thus 'in a ... desert' is expanded by one subject to 'in the middle of a ... desert'; by another to 'far out on a ... desert'. Where in the original the expressions 'a great rocket' and the witnessing 'scientists and generals' are merely juxtaposed, one subject turned this into a 'rocket towered over the many scientists and technicians below'. Equally gratuitously but with equal justification from the standpoint of orientation, the rocket was, by one subject, put 'on a launch pad pointing toward the sky'. After the firing, it was noted in the original that the rocket 'rose slowly': one subject embellished this, again with firm orientation to the earth-bound human spectator: 'the rocket blasted off, up, and away from the launch pad'. Comparably, instead of merely reporting that it proceeded to 'return and plunge' as in the original, one subject wrote: 'At its peak, it reversed and plummeted downward on its journey back to earth'. A 'watching plane' in the original became 'a pilot' in a 'nearby plane' or 'aboard an airplane'.

Spontaneous alterations of this kind seem clearly to indicate a disposition on the part of the receiver of a text to identify with it and to view its phenomena from a standpoint based on experiential realism. In the present case, for example, no subject apparently chose to imagine himself watching the blast-off from the top of a tall tower or even from the monitoring aircraft that was mentioned in the text. Yet neither vantage point would have involved any very wild fantasy. There seems to be in fact a natural, almost unshakable and sincere humility in the way we relate to discourse and identify with persons in it: and this, I take it, is not unconnected with the 'sincerity conditions' of communication (cf Searle, 1979). Thus, in circumstances similar to those in the experiment just discussed, I have found subjects (British students) apparently reluctant to replicate sentences that conflict with their own world-view. Test sentences with different groups included:

(1) She lives in Manila but she's very happy.

(2) She lives in Hawaii but she's very happy.

(3) She's very rich but she's very happy.

(4) He's very boring and deeply sincere.

While (1) was 'remembered' with almost universal accuracy, in reporting (2) and (3) subjects showed a strong tendency to replace *but* by *and* or even *and so*. By contrast, there was some tendency to change the *and* of (4) to *but*. The result with (1) should not, one supposes, be seen as evidence that Manila is regarded as an unpleasant place to live in, but rather that for the average Briton, it is just neutrally a geographical location with the normal mix of happy and unhappy people; whereas Hawaii seems to be firmly associated with the sybaritic life in which unhappiness is almost inconceivable.

Taking (2) as something of a pivot in this respect, we note that, in moving from (1) to (3) and (4), we have moved also from location as relating to literal position; we are now concerned rather with cultural, attitudinal, and moral position. The 'world' around us in a more general sense; not however a necessarily figurative sense,[1] physical location being highly determinant of our cultural values. In consequence we must expect wage *levels* to be regarded as being *at rock bottom* if we are *on the shop floor* and see things from this perspective. The same wages will seem to be *skyrocketing* and liable to *drive us into the bankruptcy courts* if our point of orientation is a seat *in the board room*. Inflation which for the British seems to have been brought *down* dramatically still seems *high* to those in Japan or in Switzerland who would look with horror at their own inflation if it was half the British figure.

Yet locked though we undoubtedly are in a narrow egocentric

---

[1]As in 'His head is in the clouds', 'Their opinions are worlds apart', 'She seems to inhabit a dream world'.

world with an environment-specific, to some extent even *family-specific*, set of beliefs, viewpoints, and standards, we are nonetheless blessedly inured to making adjustments — however imperfect and however temporary. Provided adequate perspectual clues are supplied, we are very ready in our efforts to understand other environments. How is this done? Let me attempt to answer by providing an accurate but carefully stripped version of a report on the *American* economy that appeared in a *London* newspaper:

> The Department of Commerce announces that in the third quarter the economy's rate of growth has been 4.3 per cent. Other figures reported are as follows: the increase in corporate profits was 5.3 per cent, in housing starts it was 10.8 per cent, in the gross national product it was 2.1 per cent.

I think it will be agreed that accepting the correctness of the report, including its quite precise figures, would still leave the piece difficult to understand unless one were not merely an American but an American well-versed in the economics of the United States, together with the background of expectations and trends which provide a meaning and a perspective.

When we now consider the actual printed news item, we will see that it differs from the above version of it in providing — rather laboriously and repetitiously — just such orientation (*Times*, London, 21 November 1985, Finance and Industry section):

> The American economy rebounded at a faster-than-expected pace in the third quarter, growing by 4.3 per cent, largely because of sharply lower inflation, the Department of Commerce reported yesterday.
>
> Analysts had expected third-quarter growth to be disappointing, falling below the government's rough estimates in October of 3.3 per cent.
>
> Government officials released two other sets of statistics yesterday which showed renewed vigour in the economy.
>
> Corporate profits increased by 5.3 per cent in the third quarter, the biggest rise since the 6.7 per cent gains in the first quarter of 1984.
>
> In addition, US housing starts rose by 10.8 per cent last month to the highest level in more than six months.
>
> Despite the strong third quarter performance, the

gross national product has expanded by only 2.1 per
cent in the first nine months of the year.

We note first of all the general location marker: 'The *American
economy*' — desirable for the British reader though the orientation
was already doubly provided through a headline and a Washington
by-line. A comparable report in the *New York Times* could have
assumed the shared location and begun with 'The economy ...' But
it is not enough merely to warn British readers that all the economic
data that follow have to be viewed in a United States context. Each
of the figures has to be 'placed' in relation to each other, to other
possible figures, and to comparators according either to expectation
or to past performance. Thus the economy has *rebounded* and at
a *faster-than-expected pace*. The 4.3 per cent growth is placed in the
explanatory context of *sharply lower inflation*. Instead of 4.3 per cent,
a more *disappointing* growth had been *expected* by analysts who had
themselves been more pessimistic than the Government, whose own
rough estimates had been only *3.3 per cent*. The two other sets of
figures are not given as raw data: we are told in advance that they
also show *renewed vigour in the economy*. Moreover, the first of these,
the 5.3 per cent in corporate profits, is further contextualised as
the biggest rise since the 6.7 per cent recorded in 1984; and the second,
the 10.8 per cent rise in housing starts, is 'placed' by recalling that
this is the *highest level* for six months. Finally, the GNP percentage
is not given as a mere accompaniment of these hopeful signs: it is
explicitly contrasted with them. Though the GNP has also *expanded*
it has done so by *only* 2.1 per cent.

When we are assisted in this way, and are provided with a
clear perspective, we do our best to build bridges from the location
dictated by our own parochial experience as we accommodate information of other circumstances in the wider world about us. And
it is on this propensity that planners rely when they are proposing
changes in the actual concrete world with which we are familiar.
Considering a proposal to build a tunnel between England and
France, for example, cannot be confined to the cost and mechanics
of the operation itself but must involve some imaginative grasp
of the effect the tunnel will have on people's lives and attitudes.
Equally, our willingness to engage with new perspectives can be
relied on by creators of fictitious worlds (cf Eco, 1984), whether these
purport to represent our own world with realism or whether, as
with Swift or Orwell, they seek to create for us a world that is

strikingly unlike our own:

> Behind Winston's back the voice from the telescreen
> was still babbling away about pig-iron and the over-
> fulfilment of the Ninth Three-Year Plan. The telescreen
> received and transmitted simultaneously ... There was
> of course no way of knowing whether you were being
> watched at any given moment. How often, or on what
> system, the Thought Police plugged in on any individual
> wire was guesswork ... A kilometre away the Ministry
> of Truth, his place of work, towered vast and white above
> the grimy landscape. This, he thought with a sort of
> vague distaste — this was London, chief city of Airstrip
> One, itself the third most populous of the provinces
> of Oceania ... From where Winston stood it was just
> possible to read, picked out on [the Ministry's] white
> face in elegant lettering, the three slogans of the Party:

WAR IS PEACE

FREEDOM IS SLAVERY

IGNORANCE IS STRENGTH

Internally, the location markers and features of orientation are
familiar enough. With his back to the telescreen, it is reasonable
to imagine Winston looking through a window across 'the grimy
landscape' towards a white (and hence new) skyscraper: all the more
so, it is needless to add, if we happen to be familiar with how
Orwell's model, the University Senate House, contrasted with the
rest of Bloomsbury in the 1940s. The 'elegant lettering' would of
course have to be rather large to be legible a kilometre away, but
not so implausible as to make us stumble.

Against this background of fairly familiar spatial relations,
we have a perspective from which to view something which is
shockingly very far from familiar. Mapped on to the well-known
real-world place London, we find the outlines of a nightmare world.
London is not the capital of England, nor the capital even of some
other independent country: merely the chief city of a province
— a province, what is more, that has no greater dignity and function than an airstrip. In this unfamiliar province of an unfamiliar
'Oceania', distances are measured with the unfamiliar kilometre unit:
but far greater than anything that kilometres can measure is the
terrible leap into a world of Thought Police, a Big Brother camera
in every apartment, a cynical Ministry of Truth inculcating the most

vicious of brainwash falsehood.

So familiar has *1984* now been for more than a generation, we find it almost as difficult to experience the terrible shock of discovering this new world as we do in exploring the fantasy lands invented by Jonathan Swift. Let us therefore turn to what may for most people be an unfamiliar experience of an unfamiliar world. In 1980 there appeared a novel called *The New Gulliver* by Esmé Dodderidge. This is the story of a lone survivor from a spaceship who finds himself, on recovering consciousness, in a radically strange environment — as we should expect in a country called Capovolta. By the time our hero has been taught the local language, Mr Gulliver Jr has made some observations about the cultural distance between this strange world and his own (which is of course also ours). Household work seemed to be done by men rather than by women, for example; women's dress comprised long tubular garments which 'avoided the outline of the bosom or buttocks'. But these are the merest external hints of the upside-down world with which he has soon to come to terms. The primacy of women in the professions, in exercising initiative and authority of all kinds, is reflected in such details as oaths being directed at female deities ('Great Mother, Klemo, don't speak like that ...') or the feminine pronouns being used generically:

> ... in a truly democratic society such as ours, it is not
> considered right to employ other people to perform for
> us the tasks which should be the personal responsibility
> of each individual to do for herself.

Until we come to the assumptions quietly revealed in that final pronoun, we, the non-Capovoltan readers, are tempted to feel perfectly at home in what we are thereby invited to regard as the conventionally specious talk of Western liberalism, pretending an egalitarianism whose concept of equality is conditional upon the implicit acceptance of the male as the determining norm.

It is difficult for Gulliver (who is given the name Klemo by the Capovoltans) to find anyone unprejudiced enough to discuss this gynocratic society in terms that he can regard as dispassionate and objective. When he asks why young men predominated in lowly forms of employment but seemed seldom to reach senior posts, he is told that marriage and family obligations — which affected men more than women in this society — were indeed more disruptive of men's careers than women's. In talking to a man called Tsano with whom he makes friends, he is able to ask more frankly why there was such blatant, if covert, discrimination against men:

> 'Why can't each person be judged on individual merit?'
>
> 'I suppose that would undermine the whole structure of our society, wouldn't it? I mean, some men would be doing women's work and some women doing men's.'
>
> This made me explode. 'Really, Tsano. *Who* is this authority that decides what is "women's work"; and what is "men's work"? Why can't we all do whatever it is we are most suited to do and share it all out more fairly?'
>
> 'Klemo, please', he said unhappily, 'don't sound so *angry*. I can't do anything about it, and *you* can't do anything about it. It's just the way the world is.'

The irony of this closing reference to location is of course obvious. All the arguments, Ms Dodderidge is saying, are the same as are used by apologists for an unchanging *male* supremacy in the other 'world', the only world known to the reader. Later, when Klemo has married a woman who is naturally unshakably imbued with the culture and mores of her world, quarrels break out whenever her struggling 'houseman' (a Capovoltan term corresponding in more ways than one to our 'housewife') contrasts his new environment with the one in which he was brought up:

> 'You must forgive me ... It is the custom of my country.'
>
> '*Your* country! *Your* country! Look, Klemo, I am tired of hearing about how things are in your country. I do not at all like the things you have told me about it, in any case: it sounds a vulgar and degraded place to me, and you would do better to start thinking about Capovolta as *your* country now. As my husband, you have been honored by having Capovoltan nationality bestowed upon you, and the least you can do in return is to accept gratefully the superior way of life to which it entitles you.'

This brings them no nearer to domestic bliss, however, and there comes a day when the wife comes home from work and is outraged to find Klemo plaintive and exhausted by his 'houseman's' work. She bursts into a vituperation that is an embarrassing reminder to us all of the converse situation in our own world:

> 'Great Mother!' shouted Bran. 'There's never any
> peace in this house. Either the wretched children are
> crying or you are complaining about being tired or their
> being sick. What a place to come home to!'

There is much else in this novel that is of interest in considering
the ways in which discourse can place us in another world. But
of course this need not be for satirical purposes as in Swift, Orwell,
or Ms Dodderidge. Science fiction is a common mode, and its abiding interesting is shown by the ease with which a famous example
like *The Invisible Man* of H.G. Wells can be recalled by two words
in an advertisement: as we saw in the first lecture.

But with the extraordinary developments in such fields as bio-
technology, electronics, and space exploration, the distance between
fiction and the frontiers of reality (though not perhaps between
fiction and ordinary human experience) has narrowed sharply. Who
would have thought that the Star Wars of video games a year or
so ago would have been high on the agenda of grimly serious talk
between Mr Gorbachev and President Reagan in November 1985?
Language referring to dimensions, concepts, artefacts can as easily
be describing actual experience as they can the products of inven-
tive fancy. Let us look at two passages. First:

> Sunrise has just come up behind in the periscope ... as I
> looked back out of the window, I had literally thousands
> of small luminous particles swirling round the capsule.

This happens not to be science fiction; it is unscripted natural
description from out in space on board Mercury 'Friendship Seven'
by Commander John Glenn on 20 February 1962, adapting earth-
bound locatives (the sun coming 'up', the speaker looking 'back out
of the window') for a previously unimagined and still almost totally
uncharted airless, sandless desert: in which we find ourselves, quite
literally, without perspective. And now the second:

> 'Your trouble, Dr Morgan', said the man in the wheel-
> chair is that you're on the wrong planet.'
> 'I can't help thinking', retorted Morgan, looking point-
> edly at his visitor's life-support system, 'that much the
> same may be said of you.'
> The Vice-President (Investments) of Narodny Mars

gave an appreciative chuckle.

'At least I'm here only for a week — then it's back to the Moon, and a civilised gravity. Oh, I can walk if I really have to: but I prefer otherwise.'

'If I may ask, why do you come to Earth at all?'

'I do as little as possible, but sometimes one has to be on the spot. Contrary to general belief, you can't do everything by remotes ...'[1]

This time, fiction of course. Beside the ironic reference to 'general belief' (inviting, from this mid-21st-century standpoint, contrast with the ever-expanding 'general belief' in the reader's ordinary 20th-century world), we have casual reference to a telecommunications wonder by which a screenless image of a 'remote' colleague could be speaking, full-size, in one's presence. But apart from this, we have spatial allusions (location on the Moon, on Earth, on Mars) couched in language as familiar as though we were discussing Singapore and London. The visitor looks forward to returning to a civilised *gravity* as the Singaporean in London would look forward to returning to a civilised *climate*. And just as one from the tropics can be expected to need special clothing in facing the meteorological rigours of northern Europe, so our education, our second-hand experience of real space travel, can be relied on to help us imagine the 'life-support system' required by someone trying to cope with the leaden weight of earth's gravity after being used to the Moon or Mars.

With science fiction, as with exotic satire, our locative and experiential adjustment is in fact fairly easy. In both genres, the writer is either studiously building upon the foundations of actual scientific knowledge and speculation, or is creating a world with fundamentally familiar characteristics but displaying one-for-one inversion of correlative assumptions. Creative work in surrealist modes, the grotesque, the absurd, can present far greater challenges in orientation: and this is true in verbal art as it is in painting. There have been numerous brilliant examples within recent generations of texts that have made heavy demands on the ability of readers imprisoned in a mass-production world to extricate themselves with the crampons, ropes, and toeholds of linguistic mountaineering. One cannot therefore pretend that any example within the spectrum extending from Tolkien to Samuel Beckett or Joyce could be representative. Certainly not *Finnegan's Wake*, on which I could be

---

[1] A.C. Clarke, *The Fountains of Paradise* (London: Pan Books, 1979).

tempted to focus. So let us be content with a curiosity of the post-war literary scene, the *Titus Groan* trilogy,[1] by a man who was born in the Orient and received his early education in Tientsin: Mervyn Peake. Consider the very first paragraph of this immense 1200-page novel:

> Gormenghast, that is the main massing of the original stone, taken by itself would have displayed a certain pon-derous architectural quality were it possible to have ignored the circumfusion of those mean dwellings that swarmed like an epidemic around its outer walls. They sprawled over the sloping earth, each one half way over its neighbour until, held back by the castle ramparts, the innermost of these hovels laid hold on the great walls, clamping themselves thereo like limpets to a rock. These dwellings, by ancient law, were granted this chill intimacy with the stronghold that loomed above them. Over their irregular roofs would fall throughout the sea-sons the shadows of time-eaten buttresses, of broken and lofty turrets, and, most enormous of all, the shadow of the Tower of Flints. This tower, patched unevenly with black ivy, arose like a mutilated finger from among the fists of knuckled masonry, and pointed blasphe-mously at heaven. At night the owls made of it an echoing throat; by day it stood voiceless and cast its long shadow.

Relative to each other, we note, the physical features are described with quite minute detail, for all the penumbra of Gothic hyperbole around a crudely, even gruesomely, realistic core. But relative to the known world, there is no localisation whatever: not even nega-tively or inversely as with Capovolta, still less satirically as with the London of *1984*. Peake is creating a world whose relation to ours goes no further than the common possession of basic natural materials such as rock and flint; flora such as ivy; and fauna such as owls.

As the book proceeds, the cool removal of perspective, the stark dislocation from everything with which the reader is familiar, is unswervingly maintained. The two societies, the aristocratic one within the walls and the curiously artistic proletarian one of the

---

[1] The first volume was published in 1946.

mud dwellings without, observe ancient rituals and rigid mores that are both self-contained for those societies and as remote as is conceivable from the rituals and mores of the reader. In the following passage, we glimpse some of those working in the castle kitchen:

> The walls of the vast room, which were streaming with calid moisture, were built with grey slabs of stone and were the personal concern of a company of eighteen men known as the 'Grey Scrubbers'. It had been their privilege on reaching adolescence to discover that, being the sons of their fathers, their careers had been arranged for them and that stretching ahead of them lay their identical lives consisting of an unimaginative if praiseworthy duty. This was to restore each morning to the great floor and the lofty walls of the kitchen a stainless complexion. On every day of the year from three hours before daybreak until about eleven o'clock, when the scaffolding and ladders became a hindrance to the cooks, the Grey Scrubbers fulfilled their hereditary calling. Through the character of their trade, their arms had become unusually powerful, and when they let their huge hands hang loosely at their sides, there was more than an echo of the simian ... There was no expression whatever upon the eighteen faces. They were simply slabs that the Grey Scrubbers spoke from occasionally, stared from incessantly, heard with hardly ever. They were traditionally deaf. The eyes were there, small and flat as coins and the colour of the walls themselves, as though during the long hours of professional staring the grey stone had at last reflected itself indelibly once and for all.

Again we note the pedantic precision in the physical description and already, only three or four pages into the book, the sense nonetheless of our total alienation both in experience and in sympathy from the grotesquely abhorrent society and scene. Indeed the alienation proceeds in significant measure from the linguistic precision itself: what Edwin Thumboo in his introduction to *Seven Poets* (Singapore, 1973) has felicitously described as 'the sense of proportion required to maintain decorum between a subject and its mode of expression'. Thus even in the two passages quoted, the physical exoticism which effects the reader's disorientation is

matched by a linguistic exoticism: Gormenghast is not a *building*,
it is a *massing*; the hovels do not *surround* it, they constitute a *cir-
cumfusion*; the streaming moisture in the kitchen is not *warm* but
calid, a word which collocates — if at all — with items in the lexicon of medical pathology, fittingly enough amid the images of
epidemic and mutilation. Nor is it only a matter of individual
lexical items. There is a similar clinical precision in the syntax:
elaborately textured sentences as arcane in their structure as the
alien world they describe.

Let me close this lecture on location with a third passage
from *Titus Groan*. It comes from half way through the first volume
and well illustrates the opacity of physical description in a world
from which all chance of orientation and identification is excluded:

> The roof of the Twisted Woods reflected the staring circle
> in a phosphorescent network of branches that undu-
> lated to the lower slopes of Gormenghast Mountain.
> Rising from the ground and circumscribing this baleful
> canopy, the wood was walled with impenetrable shadow.
> Nothing of what supported the chilly haze of the top-
> most branches was discernible — only a winding façade
> of blackness.
>
> The crags of the mountain were ruthless in the moon;
> cold, deadly, and shining. Distance had no meaning.

At the risk of spoiling a point already implied with sufficient force
by Peake: distance can have meaning only when it is accompanied
by perspective.

Lecture Four
Time and Tense

In stressing at the end of Lecture Three that perspective is necessary if distance is to mean anything, I was speaking with reference to the physical dislocation of Peake's Gormenghast world from our own. But in fact this is matched by a temporal dislocation. In *Titus Groan* there are no time references (nor any machines or other approximately datable artefacts or allusions) that could help us set this world in relation to, or perspective with, our own. By contrast, even disregarding the title *1984*, we are able to relate Orwell's 'chief city of Airstrip One' locationally to the known 'London', and we have a firm temporal perspective as well. Reference to 'the overfulfilment of the Ninth Three-Year Plan' tells us that it has taken twenty-seven years for this nightmare to evolve.

It would seem indeed that in human communication, 'location' in time is almost as insistently dominant as location in space. (And the metaphor of temporal 'location' is not irrelevant in this connection.) We need the contrast of *now* and *then* as we need that of *here* and *there*. Nor are their interrelations to be ignored: there is a polarity which invites our *here* and *now* to be congruently distinguished from a *there* and *then*. So far as the importance of spatial reference is concerned, I offered in the previous lecture some evidence from the distribution of adverbials in the Survey of English Usage corpus. We can do likewise with time. Again using the most numerous class of adverbial realisations, the prepositional phrase, it appears that such adverbials having temporal reference constitute about fifteen per cent of all occurrences: little more than half the figure for locatives, but still impressively high considering the large number of other semantic relations expressed by adverbials.

But, as with indicators of place, temporal reference can be realised by other linguistic means than adverbials. Consider the following variants on an expression of temporal duration:

You will be travelling *for two hours*. (adverbial)

The journey will require *two hours*. (object)

Your travelling time will be *two hours*. (complement)

Two hours will be needed for the journey. (subject)

Again as with locatives, temporal references may be *absolute* or *relative*:

I was in Geneva in October 1985.

I was in Geneva a month before the Reagan-Gorbachev summit.

Moreover, spatial measure may be expressed in terms of temporal measure (cf the etymology of *journey*). A villa near Graz may be located as *two hours' drive from Vienna*, and indeed, with extremely long distances, time-based reference is normal:

The nearest star is about ten light-years from the earth.

These observations by no means exhaust the interactions between temporal and spatial expression. We have already noted the metaphor 'temporal location', and human beings seem to find it difficult to refer to time without drawing upon the analogy of physical space:

{ She was born in Paris.
{ She was born in 1950.

{ They walked from the hotel to the library.
{ They walked from dawn to dusk.

{ I drove for 150 kilometres.
{ I drove for two hours.

{ He stopped at the street corner.
{ He stopped at noon.

Compare also the temporal use of *here* and *there* in a sentence like: 'Well, *here* we are *in 1984*, so let's compare what 1984 seemed likely to be back *there* when Orwell's book was published *in 1949*'. Of course there are spatial items such as *under, over, before, after, behind* in which the temporal usage shows less direct parallelism, and there are time-specific items such as *till, until, during*. Moreover, there are notable respects in which time is both conceptualised and linguistically represented differently from place. For example, with locative relations it is we who move through space, whereas with temporal relations it is often time that is conceived as moving:

> They want us to pass quickly.
>
> They want the time to pass quickly.

But even where the separation of functions is most notable (*here, there; now, then*), the analogies are striking. Just as we saw with physical location the urge to seek an orientation with speaker or addressee, so it is with temporal location, and we find verbs, tenses, and deictics used in a clearly interdependent way:

> She lives here now but she lived there then.
>
> They have come here.
> The time has now come. } (i.e. 'towards' the speaker)
>
> They have gone.
> The time goes quickly. } (i.e. 'away from' the speaker)
>
> That road goes to the harbour; this road goes to the park.
>
> That time you lost; this time you must win.

Just such features of temporal expression, orientation, and relativity are well brought out in the opening and contextualising paragraphs of Thomas Kilroy's novel *The Big Chapel* (1971):

> The town had no remarkable history before this. This was the time from which its people would measure its age, not with the simple measurement of years, each with its balance of bad luck and prosperity, good harvest and bad winter. Instead they would say: 'Wasn't that the winter of the trouble over the Big Chapel?' ...
>
> It gave a meaning to the place in the beginning, this trouble, it gave meaning to the lives of many families, and fathers passed on their allegiance to the priest (or his enemies) to their sons, but then, as the years passed, this energy died in the place like a light going out and the town relapsed into timelessness ...
>
> But all that is well into the future. The present is the year 1871 and the years following. Let us say between 1871 and 1883 when the priest died in the home of his sister in Newtown.

This narrative has a strikingly temporal opening, not by any means because the writer wants to take us firmly back a century, but because in the uneventful history of this little town 'the trouble of the Big Chapel' stands out as a marker like a sharp peak in a dull landscape. Just as that would invite everyone to measure distances from the peak, so the Big Chapel affair invited everyone to measure time in relation to it. The fact that it is the orientation point is well brought out in the use of tense and deixis in the third paragraph quoted. What is referred to as *that* is remote from the event on which Kilroy wishes us to focus: 'that' is seen, as it were, by staring through a telescope, which is then wrenched away from us. 'The present is 1871', though this present is of course a full century before the real present of the first reader of Kilroy's narrative. For the purposes of the story, time is conceived as linear but with only part of it having landmarks that make it measurable. In Fig. 6, T1 is the time of 'the trouble' and it is the point of temporal orientation (cf Quirk *et al.*, 1985, pp. 186 ff); T2 the year of the priest's death; T3 — irrelevant to the story itself — is the reader's now, the present time: whenever the novel is read. Before T1 and after T2 the town was in a state of 'timelessness', but between T1 and T2 time was energetically measured — in relation, of course, to the 'distance' from T1.

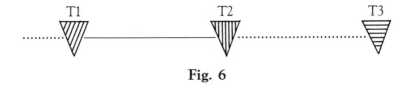

Fig. 6

The preoccupation with time in the narrative results in other nouns becoming imbued with temporal significance. A 'good harvest' connotes less the crop of grain and fruit than a unit of time or a calendar point; bad luck, prosperity, even 'the trouble' itself are used as temporal markers: a *time* of bad luck, of prosperity, the *time* when 'the trouble' occurred.[1] The bequeathing of their allegiance from father to son is matched by the movement of time (and the verb *pass* is used for both); death, the starkest time marker of all,

---

[1] Cf Dylan Thomas's propensity to 'create' temporal words and measures: 'all the *sun* long', 'a *grief* ago'. But it is a propensity widely shared: *since Camp David* — 'since the (signing of the) agreement at Camp David'; *before Sharpeville* — 'before the violence at Sharpeville'.

is reflected in these passings and made explicit in the reference to energy 'dying'.

A special aspect of time considered (and expressed) as though it were a spatial dimension is to see it as a string on which events are threaded like beads. Thus:

> Alex went to live in Manchester and bought a car. He courted a young woman named Penelope, but she came to prefer a friend of his.

Here four events are seen as discrete entities, ordered one after the other and purporting to represent their corresponding sequence in time. The linguistic sequence of independent (including co-ordinate) clauses is thus seen as an icon of temporal sequence: 'first this happened, then this, then this, ...' Moreover, this highly simplistic view of events in time is aided and abetted by the fact that the tense and aspect system of English (and many other languages) encourages us to regard one verb form as referring in a similar way to any other verb form. To put it differently and more technically, our verb forms tend to make us think of time as *topological* rather than *metrical* (cf Grimes, 1975). Thus it is only from our common-sense and experience that we might put different metrical values upon the actions represented by the four verbs in the passage quoted: *went, bought, courted, came (to prefer)*. This mismatch between language and experience is further exemplified in our single central interrogative word with respect to time, *when* (the range of which is interestingly matched locatively by *where*):

(1) When did Alex go to live in Manchester?

(2) When did he buy the car?

(3) When did he court Penelope?

(4) When did she come to prefer his friend?

A topological concept is reasonable enough for the first two, and we might receive answers such as 'In 1984' or 'In March 1984' or even 'On 14 March 1984'. But it is not reasonable for the second two. At (3), an addressee might hesitate and ask for clarification:

> Do you mean *from when till when* or *when did he start*?

Or the answer might assume one or other interpretation:

> The whole of the summer and autumn of 1984

(thus assuming that a 'metrical' question was meant);

> Well, it started sometime in the early summer, I think

(the form of the answer conveying that, even viewed topologically, 'starting to woo' cannot usually be pinpointed in time). With (4) likewise, it is improbable that even the young lady would be able to put a precise date on an 'event' which of its nature — whatever the language might suggest — is inherently gradual.

A linear textual sequence need not of course match a temporal sequence. Grammatical subordination enables us to report subsequent events before previous one:

> Alex bought a car after he went to live in Manchester

and in English we may — in some other languages, we must — clarify the temporal order by replacing the past with anterior reference by the pluperfect ('after he had gone'). In any case, sequence of events is not merely a matter of their order in time. We are disposed to view 'sequence' as 'consequence': 'post hoc' is equated with 'propter hoc'.[1] Thus in the following example, while we fully appreciate the temporal sequence, we find it difficult not to presume a causal relation also:

> Sabena moved into her friend's apartment a week after
> her father re-married.

Whether a narrative is set in the future (as with Orwell's *1984* or Burgess's *1985* or Huxley's *Brave New World*) or in the past (as with Kilroy's *The Big Chapel*), the writer operates with past tenses:

> Winston *kept* his back turned ...
>
> The parish priest ... *defied* his bishop ...

But the writer must always bear in mind the 'now' of the reader together with the 'then' of the narrative. This is particularly important where there is a striking difference between the *now* and the *then* in question, and where a large part of the narrative's purpose

---

[1]Contingent functions of various kinds commonly overlay both temporal and locative items:

> *When/Where* you find yourself in difficulties, please phone me.
> She moved to Florida *where* it was warmer.
> *Now* that I'm here, let me tell you the whole story.

(as in *1984*) is to emphasise this difference. It becomes more complex where the *now* and *then* contrast is accompanied by a sharply polarised *here* (the reader's 'here') and *there*. This is the situation when describing events in societies radically different from our own both in place and time: for example, in Frank Yerby's *The Man from Dahomey* (1971) which is set far away from familiar Europe in a West African kingdom in 1830. Yerby is aware that his readers must be assisted to relate their *now* both to what they know of the 1830 *then* in their own (especially British) society and to the 1830 *then* of a previously unknown society. Contrast:

Hwesu walked slowly to his compound

(where the past refers to a simple topological event in the narrative)

Kings of Dahomey exercised supreme control over life and death

(where an otherwise comparable past tense has a metrical value and is particularly concerned to contrast the Dahomey *then* with the reader's *now*). At times, Yerby is more overt in the latter connection. Hwesu is about to marry the King of Dahomey's daughter. We are told that she looks at him with frank desire as the ceremony proceeds. She would, Yerby feels it necessary to comment, 'have been astonished ... at the belief of her European contemporaries ... that a woman was not supposed to enjoy sex'. In switching the reader's orientation from the 1830 *then* of Dahomey to the European *then* of the same period, Yerby hopes to make his story temporally more comprehensible. But lest an 1830 British *then* was too unfamiliar to readers, he makes a direct address to them: 'be it recalled that a girl named Victoria would within a very few years occupy the British throne'. Rather clumsily and perhaps over-securely (not to mention inaccurately), the reader's orientation is now ensured: Dahomey *then* observed sexual mores of a kind that would not become familiar in Britain until long after the 'Victorian' era: which had not at this time even begun.

The need for re-orientation of one's viewpoint to more than one *then* simultaneously is something we daily confront. Consider the following:

(1) My father gave me this book.
(2) My father became blind at the age of eight.

(3) My father married my mother in Delhi.

With (1) we have no problem: when he gave me the book he was already my father. But with (2) we have two distinct *then*'s: A boy became blind and then several years later became my father. In (3), the ordinary interpretation is again to refer to two different times: A man and woman married in Delhi and some time later they became my parents. But there is nothing implausible about a meaning more like that of (1).

As we see here with *my*, a problem readily arises inasmuch as viewpoint is always in terms of a first-person observer: an 'I'. And in fact every 'I' has a longitudinal dimension determined by time and the changes that time brings with it. The following sentence is more complex than it may appear on first reading:

> Mrs Kim seemed very austere when I met her first
> some ten years ago, but now I find her warm-hearted
> and sympathetic.

Who has changed? The eye that sees belong to an 'I' whose eye it is. In John Updike's reflections on maturity (*Midpoint*, 1969), he ironically points out the danger of 'an untoward faith in the eye/I pun' (cf also Eco, 1984). So here we need to appreciate that it was to *me*, with *my* eyes of ten years ago, that Mrs Kim seemed austere. She may have changed or my outlook on people may have changed (or both), between then and now.

The position is in fact even more complex than this, and every 'I' is conscious of a multiple personality in two quite distinct ways. One is on the longitudinal time dimension already discussed; as though there were a long regression of *I*'s, one behind another. The aged *I* is conscious of the school child *I* and of an indefinite number of *I*'s in between. The other multiple personality is simultaneous in time: the *I* who is a kind parent, a jealous wife, a penny-watching shopper, a generous supporter of Oxfam; as though there were a row of *I*'s, side by side. 'I would love to own a house, but *at the same time*', we say, 'I would hate the responsibilites I'd be faced with'. (See further, Lyons, 1977.)

Anthony Powell's twelve-volume *A Dance to the Music of Time* presents a good example of where a reader is necessarily much occupied with the 'one behind another' concept of multiple personality. For example, in *Temporary Kings* the author ponders on the role of reunion dinners in adjusting views of the 'same' person.

They 'gave the chance of indulging in ... reminiscent scrutinies'. Such reunions are particularly traumatic when they bring together as civilians men who served together as soldiers. The very first such meeting, says Powell, 'revealed the gap, instantaneously come into being on demobilisation, between what was [i.e. what was *now*] and what, only a moment before, had been'.

Speaking in the same volume about another colleague whose activities had radically changed with changes in his career: 'he was no longer Books-do-furnish-a-room Bagshaw of ancient days, but Lindsay Bagshaw, the television "personality" ... He suggested a visit to his own house, something never before put forward. In the past, a pub would always have been proposed. Bagshaw himself was a little sheepish about the change.'

In Saul Bellow's novel *Humboldt's Gift* (1975), it is the *I*-figure himself whose time-separated personality and fortunes are under scrutiny. The whole narrative is a shuttling between two *then*'s: one the reader's *now* involving the narrator (Charles Citrine) and Renata; the other *then* some years earlier, involving the narrator and Humboldt, and this is interwoven as a series of 'flashbacks' occupying a large, if intermittent, part of the book as a whole. Most interestingly, it is revealed to us just why, from time to time, some event in the more recent *then* evoked the memory of the remoter *then*.

But let me turn to a historical narrative in which there is a particularly striking and ambitious consideration of the 'one behind another' personality. It is Dan Jacobson's *Rape of Tamar* (1970) where an *I*-narrator directly addresses the reader, displaying full awareness of the reader's *now* while telling a story of his involvement in events with a sharply different cultural setting in a *then* thousands of years before. Recognising that both he and the reader will have problems, since 'it's always difficult to take the dead quite seriously', he goes on:

> ... allow me to introduce myself. My name is Yonadab.
> Not a common name nowadays: at least in this part of the world. But some of you, a few of you, will have heard of me. I come from a most distinguished family.

The narrator is thus the ghost of one of King David's nephews, able to speak across the millennia and in dry ironic tones to show his orientation to the *now* and *here* of the reader ('nowadays ... in this part of the world') as well as assist in the reader's task of orientation to the *then* and *there* of David's Israel:

> You see, I can't pretend to be one of your anonymous
> narrators ... I am (or I was) the nephew of a king, the
> cousin of another, the uncle of a third ... The name
> Yonadab may mean nothing to you: but you all know
> of David, Solomon, Absalom, and many others among
> my kinsmen.
>
>   However, please don't let these names overawe you.
> I'm sure even the most plebeian among you will have
> little difficulty in recognising the conflicts and motives
> I'll have to speak of in the course of this narrative. In
> fact, if I sometimes feel embarrassed at the thought of
> how remote and archaic much of my story may appear
> to be, I am equally embarrassed at other times by how
> commonplace, how drearily familiar, you will find it
> all. Fraternal rivalries, incestuous desires, the struggle
> between a father and his sons, the greed for possessions
> and power ...

Part of the orientation lies in the unending truism that however
far the reader is from the *then* and *there* of the story, the human
predicament is ever recognisable; plus ça change ... Moreover, by
repeatedly switching between present and past in relation to himself ('I am (or I was) the nephew of a king') in both recalling the
shame of the rape and feeling it again 'now' at the moment of
narration, the *I*-figure is protesting this unchanging continuity.
The 'one behind another' image is relevant only insofar as Yonadab
can now see himself and the events in the different context and
circumstances of 'you', the readers.

   And even with *you*, Jacobson contrives to make us understand
that the passage of time and the passage through space have made
little difference. He uses the *you* pronoun, as we have seen, to
address the initially puzzled readers of the late twentieth century.
His studiously informal style allows him to use *you* also as the
indefinite pronoun (only very roughly equivalent to 'one'). Recalling his experience of David in the throne-room, all couched in the
timeless present of background description, the narrator tells us:

> He is a master of surprise and duplicity; gentle when
> you expect him to be stern, savage when you expect
> him to be indulgent ...

But within a few lines, the *you* pronoun changes its reference —
twice:

> ... unfamiliar when you expect him to be aloof. And
> that's not all, by any means. You must admit, for exam-
> ple, that it's not a small achievement to have your
> enemies killed off by your henchmen, as any tyrant
> would, and then to win for yourself a reputation as
> a man of honour and tender conscience — how? By
> killing, in a fit of outraged sensibility, those who have
> done the job for you! Yet David has pulled off that
> particular trick more than once ...

In the first line above, we continue the string of indefinite *you*
occurrences. In the second line, however, *you* is addressed to the
twentieth-century reader who is being given this account of life
in David's court. From then on *your* and *you* refer to a putative
tyrant who is finally of course identified with David.

Now here we have a texture with complexity of a very high
order. The frequent use of *you* addressed to the readers is relatively
unambiguous, though the effect is to drag us all back, to suck us
all in, to the sordidness, the tension, the fears, and the cruelty of
David's court. The indefinite *you* begins as any representative of
those who were obliged to attend the court and live in David's
power: particularly the representative who is telling us the story.
We are very conscious of being told what 'I Yonadab' felt as 'I'
carefully observed my powerful uncle's behaviour ('The rest of *us*
remain in the throne room ... discussing what *we* have just seen
and heard'). But as we readers become involved, *you* the indefinite
witness embraces us too: and this is enhanced by the occasional
cunning switch ('You must admit') where only the readers can
be meant. Most cunningly of all, the *you* as the type of tyrant,
innocently projected at one moment as anyone in that particular
position and then explicitly identified with the uniquely arbitrary
David, disturbingly suggests identification both with us as readers
and with (of course) Yonadab himself. The reader's orientation with
the *then* and *there* of the narrative is all too complete for comfort.
We see now a more sinister reason for the narrator's apology at
'the thought of how remote and archaic much of my story may
appear to be' though also of 'how commonplace, how drearily
familiar, you will find it all'. We see also a more sinister reason for
those pages of present tenses. Have they been merely to distinguish

background generalities, the broad scene-setting, from the topological sequence of events constituting the story of the rape? Or are they present tenses that insist on the 'drearily familiar' involvement of us all in just such brutalities? The ghost and David and we readers are gathered together into one time and place: here and now.

Let us look at little more closely (if less grippingly) at this present/past distinction. It is perhaps useful to distinguish between verbal tenses as being either *experiential* or *speculative*. It is no accident that in English, as in so many languages, there is a clear and regular morphological relation between present and past; as in

> I played squash yesterday.
>
> I play squash every day.

but not between these and the 'future':

> I'll play squash tomorrow.
>
> I'm going to play squash tomorrow.
>
> I may play squash tomorrow.
>
> I hope to play squash tomorrow.

The future tense is thus made up of volition, intention, possibility: in a word, speculation. The present and past are what we know: by experience. Yet these, the past and the present, are on a very different footing from each other. Provided there are no special indications to the contrary,[1] a past tense will indicate that the event has both taken place and that a time gap has elapsed between this event and the present, our 'now'. This will be true whether the verb has inherent 'punctual' meaning or inherent 'durative' meaning:

> (1) I lost my umbrella.
>
> (2) I lived in India.

In (1) 'at some time in the past' is entailed with no implication that it is still lost; in (2) '*for* some time in the past' is entailed but with the corollary that I do not still live there. In short, the past tense has specific time reference.

---

[1]Notable cases of such 'special indications' include the use of the past for what purports to be remote through its implausibility ('If I *believed* that, I would believe anything') or through courteous reluctance to intrude: 'I *wanted* to ask if you will support my application', 'I *wondered* whether you are free for a moment'.

By contrast, the morphologically related present tense (*I lose*, *I live*) has no specific time reference. In consequence, an instantial example of events expressed in the present will typically employ the past:

> I *lose* my umbrella quite often because I *pay* a large number of visits every day. I *leave* it behind and then *have* no idea where it *is*. For example, last month I actually *left* it in a Lost Property Office where I *went* to inquire about some missing keys.

In thus being concerned with general conditions, 'undated', the present tense has little natural place in narrative, though a prominent one in description; for example, in scientific description:

> It is well-known that shot-peening *protects* metals against stress corrosion cracking. It now appears that high-intensity peening of stainless steel also *prevents* inter-granular corrosion cracking. When certain steels are sensitised by heating, chromium carbides *precipitate* along continuous grain boundaries. As a result, inter-granular corrosion *starts* in the depleted surface areas and *propagates* down ...

It will be noticed that I am ignoring the means by which in English we can refer to events in present time with the same discreteness with which we refer to past events by means of the past tense. Compare the following telephone message:

> I saw your sister on television at 10 p.m. last night and now it's again 10 p.m. so *I'm telephoning* to say that *I'm watching* the same programme and *I'm hoping* to see her again.

The tense-reference analogy is there, but significantly the formal correspondence is not; a different morphological system is involved.

Of course, the present (as distinct from this 'progressive', sometimes called 'continuous' form) has a place in some forms of narrative too. For example, in simultaneous reportage, especially of sport:

> Davis walks to the far end, bends over the table, pauses. He chalks his cue, stoops to sight his shot again, slides the cue gently back and forth; pauses again.

There is also the 'historic' present, with past-time reference, and often used at points of narrative excitement in alternation with the more usual past-tense verbs:

> The house was surrounded and the police were content to wait. Occasionally the lights from a passing car revealed the locked gate and the empty driveway. Otherwise everything lay in darkness and in silence. Suddenly a light appears in an upstairs room; then a window opens and a figure is clearly visible in silhouette.

But these are exceptional and relatively minor uses of the present; in general the occurrence of the present invites interpretation in relation to the *timeless truth* of experience rather than the *instantial 'accident'* of experience. So it is when we refer to a work of art in contrast to the process of its creation:

(1) Gavin Douglas wrote *The Palace of Honour* in about the year 1500.

(2) He dedicated it to King James the Fourth of Scotland.

(3) In it, Douglas demonstrated his love of pageantry.

(4) The poem was written in rhyming couplets.

(5) The work has clear affinities with much of Chaucer's romantic poetry.

(6) The poem deals with themes long-since become unfashionable.

In moving from past tenses to present, we distinguish between historic events, now clearly spearated from us, as in (1), to permanent features in a poem that still exists, as in (6). In neither (1) nor (6) could the tense be changed, but between these extremes the forms selected are not obligatory, and it is of some interest to consider the effects of switching the tenses. Replacing *has* by *had* in (5) would narrow the observation to the impression which the poem had upon readers in Douglas's own time: they *noted* the Chaucerian affinities. By contrast, where (4) is simply the passive of the historic statement that Douglas *wrote* the poem in couplets, a switch to the present would turn the statement into a description of the poem's metre as observed by any reader — today or at any other time. Replacement of past by present in (2) and (3) makes the statements seem superficially like 'historic present' narrative, but here again we are concerned rather with disjoining the poem from the time of its composition and we entail that the poem is still in existence: we are not merely referring to known facts about a past work.

In thus connoting what is not tied to some particular event and time, the present has a perfectly rational role in stage directions:

> The lights come up to reveal YAKOV ... Beside him
> stands DR TRILETZKY, a match in his hand ... There
> is a smell of sulphur in the air. The rocket bursts off
> and the stick falls into the garden. YAKOV backs away
> towards the house in alarm ...[1]

By contrast, with reference to any one production of the play, it could be reported that 'The lights *came* up. Beside Yakov *stood* Triletzky. There *was* a smell of sulphur ...' The convention of stage directions is to describe the permanent truth that these things happen whenever the play is produced. Such a 'scene-setting' function of the present is doubtless part of what helps us to accept it, even for specific historic events, in newspaper headlines. Thus on the front page of *The Times* on 26 November 1985, the headline

> Egypt hints at link with Libya

is immediately followed by the report with normal past-tense verbs:

> Egypt hinted yesterday that the gunmen who seized one
> of its airliners had links with Libya ...

We are now in a better position to look again at the use of tenses in Jacobson's *Rape of Tamar*:

> At last the king stands and makes his way out of the
> room ... The rest of us remain in the throne-room for
> a while ... our gestures are a little freer ... now that we
> are rid of the restraint ... Then we begin to drift out ...

The verb forms convey some sense of the immediacy and tension associated with the historic present, but in fact they relate to a permanent or at any rate habitual and typical state of affairs. Explicitly.

---

[1]Michael Frayn, *Wild Honey*, translated and adapted from Chekhov (London: Methuen, 1984).

The parts I have quoted are accompanied by such expressions as 'almost always' and 'usually', which I suppressed. Moreover, the dramatic analogy of 'scene-setting' is made explicit too:

> My subject being what it is, my *characters* being what they are, I expect you [i.e. narrator speaking to reader] would welcome a formal court *scene* before we [i.e. narrator and reader] go any further.

The italics are of course mine, but they are scarcely necessary since the metaphor is well endorsed:

> Yet what a strange show it is, all said and done: this drama whose very point it almost invariably is that there should be no drama ... I am now condemned to be a stage-manager to phantoms; an annalist (analyst?) of apparitions ...

The pun here superbly captures the ambiguities in which we have become enmeshed: the variable reference of *you*, the variable reference of the present tenses, the metaphor of dramatic production. Just as Updike hints that the homophony of *I* and *eye* is not arbitrarily coincidental, so here we find Jacobson suggesting that one cannot be an annalist without being in part an analyst too. Events can occur simultaneously in time: and they may or may not be otherwise related. Events can follow each other in sequence and they may or may not be otherwise related.

But as we have seen repeatedly in this lecture, we are not disposed to disregard the possibility of such other relations, the possibility that post hoc is propter hoc. We are not disposed to regard time or the passage of time as being without the profoundest influence on our lives and the attitudes which inform our lives.

Significantly, at the point where (after fifteen or sixteen pages of preliminaries) Jacobson settles in to treat his story as annals, as events in time well suited to past-tense treatment, he not merely adopts past-tense narration but — with another informal pun — makes a direct allusion to the role of time in this or any other narrative:

> But of Tamar, his sister, [Amnon] did not speak at all until the night on which I suppose it can be said our story properly begins (and about time too!)

Lecture Five
Organisation: Content and Presentation

In the first lecture, we discussed our dependence in any communication on our assumptions about the kind, degree, and limits of knowledge held in common between author and addressee. In the second, we went on to consider how we moved from a base of assumed 'shared knowledge' to make observations that would be new and interesting to the addressee. In my third and fourth lectures, we explored this common base with particular reference to the need for providing the addressee with locational and temporal orientation, so that a bridge may be built across from the addressee's *here* and *now* to whatever *there* and *then* may be entailed by the discourse.

It must surely be clear that all of this is not merely relevant to the subject of the present lecture in a preparatory way: rather, it goes a long way to providing the actual framework of textual organisation which is now our concern. In other words, we have already established important basic parameters of organisation, and, as a means of examining these and further theoretical aspects of structure in more detail, it may be useful to study a text which we can for our present purposes regard as complete and self-contained. From it we shall first derive the bare bones of content which it has been the author's task to communicate. Then we shall look at the textual procedures he has used in effecting this task.

From one point of view, the choice of text is unimportant. As I hope has been made clear, all communications — spoken or written, practical or fictive — are of profound interest: though of course not necessarily of equal interest. I have chosen a written text rather than a spoken one, not because writing is more typical (the converse is overwhelmingly true) but because it presents a form that is more accessible to study, as anyone will know who has analysed samples of spontaneous talk. Moreover, while choosing a written text that I hope will be of some general interest, I have sought a piece of writing relatively remote from my own professional concern with English literary and linguistic studies. Instead, its domain is that relatively new area in electronic technology known as artificial intelligence, and the author — though a highly experienced writer — is himself a trained and practising engineer. He is Geoffrey Simons, a man in his forties who is a senior executive in the Manchester headquarters of the National Computing Centre. The text appeared in the first issue of *The Decision Maker*, published in London in August 1985. It well illustrates the tenet that every communicative task, however mundane and practical, merits careful shaping by the communicator's art — and merits equally the addressee's critical attention (cf Enkvist, 1986):

> Any patient who tells his doctor he wants a second opinion can expect the atmosphere in the surgery to chill noticeably. It is, after all, an expression of lack of confidence in the doctor's ability to make a sound and accurate judgement. Few people can help but feel resent-   5
> ful at such an attack on their professional ability.
>
> What doctors and executives of all kinds may have to come to terms with in the not too distant future, however, is a permanent second opinion on their desk tops in the form of 'expert systems' — computer pro-   10
> grams which go a long way towards emulating the thinking processes of the best human brains in a particular area of expertise.
>
> To make effective use of these powerful new decision-making tools, professionals and leaders may have to   15
> change ideas about computers radically. Currently, we tend to view the business computer as merely a glorified calculator, able to do a few useful tricks such as word processing. Already, however, many executives are making use of this calculating ability through 'decision   20
> support systems' — powerful programs that lead them through logical steps of thinking about specific problems, until the alternative solutions and their implications are clear. It is, of course, still the executive's decision which of the various alternatives to choose.   25
>
> Expert advisory systems, sometimes referred to as 'artificial intelligence', take that all important step beyond merely guiding the decision process to actually suggesting what the correct decision should be. They allow the user to have a real dialogue with his machine,   30

which will offer advice, proffer decisions and explain the
reasoning behind its conclusions. In the years to come
we shall see a proliferation of expert systems, working
together with decision support systems to help managers
in all sorts of ways and particularly in handling the   35
complex planning and financial problems that concern
top management. There are, as yet, very few successful
expert systems in everyday operation. As a result, there
is no clear answer to the fierce debate between the sup-
pliers, who maintain that computer-based expert systems   40
are innovative and revolutionary vital management
tools; and critics, who point out that, for the moment
at least, they are pretentious and inefficient, not least
because they make very heavy demands on computer
processing time and storage capacity.   45

Another important feature of expert systems is that
they are often, though not always, equipped to deal with
'fuzzy' categories — to allow for the obvious circumstance
that much of human knowledge is partial and uncer-
tain, seemingly poorly suited to the neat categorisations   50
demanded by traditional computer systems.

Of course, most of the applications of expert systems will not affect top management directly. They will
solve problems in geology, engineering, computer design
and so on. But these applications are important to top   55
management because they will allow the organisation
as a whole to make better decisions more often.

Let us now work backwards and (as the jargon has it) 'mine'
the article for what we may deduce was the *brief* that Simons had
before him:

Announce expert systems
Location and function
Capacity: mechanical reasoning
           interactive
           incomplete data
Potential still controversial
Better with basic problems than policy decisions

It may further help us (though Simons might not have found it
necessary) to flesh this out as a continuous prose synopsis. We shall
follow the above order of items in the 'brief', but at intervals I have

inserted parenthesised line numbers which refer to the point at which in the final text the items of information are actually treated:

> Programs called 'expert systems' will soon be available for office computers (10). They will challenge executives to check their own conclusions against mechanically produced reasoned argument (32); they can be used interactively (30), and in principle can make allowance for inadequate information (49).
>
> The potential of expert systems is not yet fully demonstrable and is therefore a matter of controversy (37–39). In any case, while their value in solving basic data problems will enhance intermediate decision-making (57), they will not usually impinge directly on top management (53).

This synopsis or précis is less than a fifth of the 500 words used by Simons: a quantum which we may assume conformed with an editorial allowance to which he was working. We can now proceed to compare the final version with the synopsis in two respects: one, the material added by Simons over and above the items in his presumed remit; two, the points at which in his own elaborated version he slotted in these remitted items. In both respects we shall be assisted by the parenthesised numerals.

The earliest numbered reference in the synopsis is to line 10. This reflects the need felt by Simons to find an area of experience common to himself and all potential readers: a shared-knowledge base from which he can begin to introduce what he can safely assume will be new to the reader. He chooses to locate the reader in the tense atmosphere of a doctor's surgery where, though doubtless nervous and anxious (but as the participant who will have to bear whatever burden the decision imposes), he summons courage to seek a second opinion. But the second sentence (lines 5–6) invites the reader to switch places and to sympathise with the doctor: obviously more difficult, since while every reader will have been a patient, none using this management journal is likely to be a doctor. But difficult as it is, Simons rightly feels it is communicatively necessary, since, as the next sentence shows (lines 7–13), a new development in the New Technology is going to make every senior decision-making worker face the prospect of having his opinion challenged in this way.

Simons has thus achieved a beginning which effects a transition from a familiar situation (in a doctor's surgery) in an unfamiliar role (being the doctor) to a familiar role (executive) in an unfamiliar situation (having his opinion challenged by a machine).

But as we scrutinise the synopsis further, we find that there are no line references relating to the final version for the space of the next twenty lines. In other words, having around line 10 introduced the first and most crucial piece of new information, Simons is content to indulge in further leisurely provision of background support before tackling the next point in his 'brief.' The notion of 'expert systems' linked to the desk computer is followed not by what these 'expert systems' have to offer but by a further indulgence in shared knowledge: a recapitulation of the common uses of the desk computer as they are likely to be familiar with the reader up to the present time. We notice in this connection that the reader has been locationally moved from the doctor's surgery to his own executive office; and temporally the reader is moved from a bare glimpse of the future to a firm reminder of the present. Simons has achieved (in terms of my third and fourth lectures) a firm orientation to his reader's *here* and *now*.

With the paragraph beginning in line 26, Simons feels confident in claiming that, quantum leap or not, the transition from the more sophisticated uses of computers to the introduction of 'expert systems' is a logical and comprehensible step. He is now midway through the total space of his article, having achieved no more than an entertaining introduction in which, after a prefatory medical parable, he has embedded one important piece of new information: the advent of the 'expert systems' whose properties it is his main purpose to explore. He clearly feels that he has now securely won his reader's attention and with it an informed interest. As the synopsis shows, the second half of the article packs in new information with far greater density: though not always in the same order as in the 'brief' or in the synopsis.

The differences will repay study, provided of course we remember that they arise from the fact that one presenter (Simons) is responsible for the full text and that another (myself) is responsible for the synopsis and the 'mined' brief of which the synopsis is an expansion. It is conceivable that Simons started with a brief which laid out all points in the order found in the final version. But even so, it is worth inquiring why the point about '"fuzzy" categories' appears where it does (around line 48) and not in the section around lines 28 to 33 where the main features of 'expert systems' are set forth. Simons does after all specify it as being *another* 'important feature', thus obliging the reader to link line 46 back to this 'main features' section fifteen lines earlier.

The answer seems to lie in the writer's having had to make a choice between two incompatible desiderata — incompatible because of the necessarily linear constraints of communication. The first option was to take all the currently known features of the new systems and present them together where they logically belong (as in the synopsis), thus both bunching a great deal of new information and also postponing all of the suggested ways in which it will influence management, as well as the degree to which the new procedures are controversial. The other option was a more gradualist presentation, such as is consonant with lines 1–25, the main new features being followed by the management application, followed by the controversy and scepticism, followed by 'another' new feature, followed by the final and relatively limiting and re-strictive discussion of application. Simons chose the second of these approaches: what has been described as the 'chain' mode of rhetorical design (cf Nash, 1980).

It is of some interest to reflect that the choice may well have depended on the mere length of the exposition. If Simons' order had been adopted in the synopsis, the result would have been an ill-constructed and illogical sequence: confusing, perhaps. If the order adopted in the synopsis had been followed in the fuller version, the reader *might* have a duller, more pedantic, more pedagogical — and hence less attractive — presentation. We can be fairly sure that Simons was intent on avoiding any such general impression. He is seeking to woo his readers' interest and then to combine the teaching of new facts with the influencing of managerial attitudes.

That we can be the more confident in making this observation will emerge as we now proceed to look at the language of the piece in more detail. First, the lexicon. Though the subject is a new and rather abstruse area of computer technology, the lexicon is stu-diously general and non-specialist. At the same time, the writer is equally careful not to give the impression that he is 'talking down' to readers innocent of electronics. If anything, in suppressing his own technical knowledge, he dons the mask more congruent with the special skills of his perceived readers. As managerial executives, they will feel at home in the business ambience of *organisation, ex-pertise, management tools, systems, operation, design, dialogue,* together with such adjectives as *powerful*, *revolutionary*, and *innovative*. Above all, there are the repeated uses of the executive's key word, *decision*.

By contrast, while quietly advancing the claims of electronic potential, the associated 'high tech' lexicon is low-key. The use of *interactive* (seemingly so natural in both the brief and the synopsis) is avoided by paraphrase, and a comfortingly sympathetic relation with the non-engineer is cultivated by referring to the computer as 'a glorified calculator' performing 'a few useful tricks', and by echoing the view of some that expert systems are 'pretentious'. Not least suggestive in this connection is the use of quotation marks for terms sensitively expected to be unfamiliar (and hence in need of explicit recognition, almost of *apologetic* recognition): 'expert systems', 'decision support systems', 'artificial intelligence'. The quotation marks around 'fuzzy' may have the same value (since it is a technical term in some areas of the social sciences) but they may be apologetic in the opposite direction: recognising that the imprecise and informal connotations of the word may seem out of keeping with the generally urbane and dignified tone.

This tone is conveyed not only by the lexicon but by a grammar which equally avoids stridency, heartiness, colloquialism. Sentences are in consequence rather lengthy, fairly complex, regularly well-formed, and often with a sense of traditional rhetorical art. It is perhaps significant that this last point should be especially notable in what is arguably the key sentence of the entire piece: setting out what expert systems have to offer (lines 30–32):

> They allow the user to have a real dialogue with his
> machine, which will offer advice, proffer decisions and
> explain the reasoning behind its conclusions.

The structure of the relative clause show signs (all too clearly, a harsh critic might say) of careful planning. Triadic arrangement has a peculiar attraction in many rhetorical traditions:

> Veni, vidi, vici.
>
> Tall, dark and handsome.
>
> When the hostages were released, all were exhausted,
> some were in a state of shock, and a few showed terrible
> signs of physical injury.

Triads give the impression of expansive exposition: indeed of *complete* exposition: a string of activities, a list of properties, has conferred upon it a certain unity as well as a totality (cf Haiman, 1980). Moreover, while the items in a triad are typically co-ordinate and are also structurally parallel, they are not felt to be equal in status; rather they build up to a climax: the principle of *end-focus*. And the sense that the third item is the most important is often matched by making it the longest: the principle of *end-weight* (cf Quirk *et al.*, 1985). So in the Simons sentence we get the impression that the system's properties amount to a satisfying and impressive whole, that we have been told them all, and that the last (the reasoning) is presented as most important. And some effort has been made at a progression in importance between the first item and the second, as well as between these two and the climactic third. Advice is not only a preliminary to decision-making, but in being contributory it is inherently less important. The second member of the triad is in the correct rhetorical position, and its greater weight is (minimally) reflected in its slightly greater length and in the somewhat more impressive verb: though *proffer* strikes a perhaps unfortunate note in seeming to be a desperate attempt at 'elegant variation' and the avoidance of a repeated *offer*.

The principle of end-weight, deferring matter of heaviest linguistic substance (such as number and length of words), is appropriately matched by making end-position the point of greatest semantic and communicative weight as well. A sentence 'rheme' is thus polarised from the sentence 'theme' or 'topic' in initial position, as discussed in my second lecture. Doubtless without ever having heard of 'functional sentence perspective' (cf Firbas, 1979, 1986), Simons shows the communicator's instinct for making grammar work to this effect. Take for example (lines 5–6):

> Few people can help but feel resentful at such an attack
> on their professional ability.

Not only is the longest noun phrase put at the end; but it is this noun phrase which is communicatively climactic. Compare such paraphrases as:

> Such an attack on their professional ability cannot
> help but make most people feel resentful.

> Such an attack on their professional ability cannot help
> but cause resentment in all but a few people.

> For few people can such an attack on their professional

ability be other than a cause of resentment.

Among the grammatical devices used by Simons to achieve a rhetorical focus with end-weight is the existential *there* construction. For example, the two successive sentences in lines 37 ff:

> There are, as yet, very few successful expert systems in everyday operation. As a result, there is no clear answer to the fierce debate ...

Alternative presentations would be clumsier and more pompous, as well as being communicatively less effective in putting elements that are properly rhematic into a thematic position:

> Very few successful expert systems have been perfected as yet for everyday operation. No clear answer to the fierce debate can as a result be given.

Like existential *there*, the anticipatory *it* as subject is a convenient way of achieving a light thematic opening to a sentence with postponement of a weighty element. Simons adopts this device in lines 24–25:

> It is, of course, still the executive's decision which of the various alternatives to choose.

The logical subject is the final *which*-clause and this could equally be made the grammatical subject:

> Which of the various alternatives to choose is, of course, the executive's decision.

But this would not merely have produced an imbalance in weight (long subject, short complement) but a rhetorical imbalance also, with the important *which*-clause made inappropriately thematic.

In contrasting the existential sentences of lines 37 ff with alternative versions, the passive was introduced (*have been perfected, can ... be given*). Now, although the passive is a common feature in communications on technical subjects, it is a striking testimony to Simons' determination to write in an urbane and non-technical style that the passive scarcely occurs at all in the article. Indeed, reckoning as passive only the 'central' type (Quirk *et al.*, 1985, p. 167) which can be related to the active voice, there are only two examples, and even they are in non-finite clauses, in each case postmodifiers in noun phrases:

> ... systems, sometimes referred to as 'artificial intelligence'
> (lines 26–27)
>
> ... categorisations demanded by traditional computer
> systems (lines 50–51)

Both are well justified by the brevity they achieve. Replacement by the active would entail making the clauses finite. This would be particularly unwelcome in the former case since nothing corresponding to a plausible active subject is recoverable:

> ... systems, which *computer scientists* (?) sometimes refer
> to as 'artificial intelligence'.

In the second example, where the active subject is easy to recover from the agent phrase, replacement of the non-finite passive would frustrate functional sentence perspective in preventing the sentence from ending with the grammatically and semantically weighty element. Thus instead of the wording found in lines 50–51, we would have:

> ... categorisations that traditional computer systems
> demand.

The Simons article serves not a narrative but a descriptive purpose: descriptive moreover of a speculative future as well as of a contrasting present. Verb tenses and other time indicators range between present and future reference as appropriate. Orientation to the reader's 'now' is therefore central to the piece — and easy enough to achieve: whether by the timeless habitual present tenses referring to common experience ('Any patient who *tells* his doctor he *wants* a second opinion', 'we *tend* to view the business computer ...') or by the single example (lines 19–20) of an instantial progressive: 'many executives *are making* use ...' Supportive of and co-occurring with the present tenses, we have numerous adverbials (*currently, already, for the moment at least, as yet; sometimes, often, always*), as well as temporal premodifiers in noun-phrase structures (*traditional* in line 51, *everyday* in line 38).

Such correlates of the reader's *now* form the temporal back-cloth for staging scenes of the future. But *now* has two aspects in the context of the article: (a) familiar current practice, and (b) unfamiliar equipment already in existence but not yet exploited. The future (c) concerns changing (a) to make use of (b). Thus in projecting (c), we have present tenses relating to (b) (as in 'computer programs which *go* a long way ...', 'Expert advisory systems ... *take* that all important step ... They *allow* ... *are* often ... equipped') as well as future tenses concerning the change from (a); for example, *we shall see* (33), *will ... affect* (53), *will solve* (lines 53–54), *will allow* (56). If we now look at some of the juxtapositions of present and *will* plus infinitive, we see that more is involved than the contrast of present time and future time. In

> ... these applications *are* important ... because they *will allow* (lines 55–56)

we are indeed contrasting present evaluation ('*are* important') with future demonstration ('*will allow*'). But in lines 29–31, the same formal distinction is used to effect a different distinction:

> They *allow* the user to have a real dialogue with his machine, which *will offer* advice ...

This is more like the contrast between verb forms that we have in distinguishing from among a set of current properties a subset that is seen as very special or perhaps only potential. For example:

> I *have* a new car which *uses* very little fuel but *will tow* a heavy caravan.

> Don't you know that oil *will float* on water? Watch: a drop of cooking oil is put into this saucer of water. You see? It *is floating*.

Habitual predictive meaning can also be expressed by *can*:

> My new car *can tow* a heavy caravan.

> ... a real dialogue with his machine, which *can offer* advice ...

This use of *can* does not occur in the Simons article, which in consequence permits a doubtless valuable ambiguity to arise between projected — and quite speculative — developments that managers 'may have to come to terms with in the not too distant future' (lines 7–8) and those facilities which actually exist (machines that *can/will* do things *now*) and which managers should *already* be making it their business to understand and exploit.

With many of the selections of items and forms that we have been considering, it is unnecessary to postulate conscious planning by the author, with conscious discrete choices, as the article is being written. The instinct of a confidently practised communicator may well have sufficed. But there are aspects of the composition that are, we may agree, less likely to have been achieved unconsciously: for example, paragraph boundaries, sentence boundaries, sentence linkage, and cross-reference. Let us look at these in reverse order.

Cross-reference for intratextual connection is a frequent necessity both within and between sentences. Complete repetition of the item in question (though sometimes justifiable in legal documents) makes the communication both stylistically unpleasant and less easily assimilable. For example, let us assume that someone wrote:

> The third pilot project report was felt to be more urgent than the new research proposal and the director asked me to read the third pilot project report. After careful study, I questioned some points in the third pilot project report and suggested general ways in which the third pilot project report should be revised.

It is not difficult to produce something better without losing track on the cross-references to this heavily emphasised report:

> *The third pilot project report* was felt to be more urgent than the new research proposal and the director asked me to read *it*. After careful study, I questioned some points in *this report* and suggested several ways in which *the document* should be revised.

Three different devices are here exemplified, all of them replacing the long noun phrase by items that we can be sure of being uniquely anaphoric. In one case, we have a summary as noun reference: *this report*; in another, we have a paraphrasal allusion: *the document*; and thirdly, we have pronominalisation of the entire noun phrase: *it*. The summary is doubtless easiest to appreciate since it is most explicit: the use of the 'near' determiner *this* confirms the reader's belief that the word *report* which follows excludes any other report which he may have in mind or which the wider context may have suggested: it will be understood as 'this *recently mentioned* report. The paraphrase is only marginally more risky. Reports may be oral

as well as written and only the latter could be alluded to as a
'document'. But in the present case, reference has been made to
reading the report, so that any possibility of doubt is excluded. What
else, following this *report* in the same sentence, could *the document*
refer to? But in addition to using their common sense, readers
are inured to the device of paraphrase to avoid lexical repetition
(compare the rather obtrusive 'elegant variation' of *offer* and *proffer*
in the Simons text, line 31).

The third device, pronominalisation, is by far the commonest
and most familiar. Alone of the three we are considering, it could
have been used at all three points in the example: and this is a
measure of how inconspicuous are the so-called 'personal' pronouns,
he, she, it, they. The price we pay for the convenience of these short,
inconspicuous, lightly stressed items is that they are the least explicit, and in using them authors have to rely on both the good
sense and on the co-operativeness of their addressees. Thus in the
present example, *it* could grammatically refer to either of the two
noun phrase:

> *The third pilot project report* was felt to be more urgent
> than *the new research proposal*, and the director asked
> me to read *it*.

Indeed, proximity might argue that *the new research proposal* was
the likelier antecedent of *it*. But the writer expects the addressee
to interpret any inexplicit item in the light of the total meaning
of the text. Since one document is said here to be more urgent
than the other, it will not normally cross the addressee's mind that
the director can be referring to anything else when he asks that
it be read.

As we would expect in a text of 500 words, there is a great
deal of cross-reference in the Simons article. There is a simple instance of summary in line 55, *these applications* referring back (across
two sentence boundaries) to *most of the applications of expert systems.*
There are two quite striking paraphrases. The first example comes
in the first paragraph, where *such an attack on their professional
ability* refers back to *an expression of lack of confidence in the doctor's
ability to make a sound and accurate judgement.* It is worth noting
again that, despite its being shorter, the paraphrase makes a signal
contribution by being interpretive as well as summative: expressing
lack of confidence is reasonably seen (from the doctor's viewpoint)
as *an attack*; making sound and accurate judgements is claimed to

be a measure of a doctor's *ability*. The other paraphrase occurs in lines 14–15, where *these powerful new decision-making tools* refers back to the lengthy exposition of 'expert systems' in the previous sentence and paragraph: *computer programs which go a long way towards emulating the thinking processes of the best human brains in a particular area of expertise*. The paraphrase unambiguously cross-refers but despite being radically shorter, it is so contrived by the author as to add to the reader's knowledge by glossing and interpreting the longer exposition. Thus the programs, because of their potential, are now called *tools*; the fact that they can emulate thought is interpreted as indicating that they are *powerful*; the working of the best human and expert brains is pinpointed as *decision-making*.

But overwhelmingly the chief cross-reference device is pronominalisation — as in the very first line: '*Any patient* who tells *his* doctor *he* wants a second opinion ...' The *doctors and executives* of line 7 are referred to by *their* in line 9; and *expert systems* in line 26 are referred to by *they* in lines 29, 43, 44, 47 and 53. There is also pronominalisation by the relatives *who* (as in 40) and *which* (as in 31). It is perhaps worth pausing over one other pronoun. In line 33, *we* refers extratextually and generically: the writer invites the reader to join him and the rest of society in a prediction of what 'we' shall all witness. But the only other occurrence of *we* (in line 16) has a sharply different function. The context is this:

> ... professionals and leaders may have to change ideas
> about computers radically. Currently, we tend to view
> the business computer as merely a glorified calculator ...

The reference here is surely intratextual and indeed plainly enough anaphoric: professionals and leaders will need to change their ideas — and one of their present ideas is that a computer is just another calculator. But if this is the meaning and if this is the basis for the connection between the subjects of the two neighbouring clauses, why switch from third person (*professionals and leaders*) to first person (*we*) rather than use the grammatically regular *they*? The answer in one word is tact. The writer is criticising 'professionals and leaders' in general for their benighted views, and prefers to submit himself also to this judgement than to put himself aside and claim that it is only others ('they') who have out-dated attitudes. This, as we shall see in the next lecture, contributes to an important aspect of communication: the need to ensure the goodwill and co-operation of the addressee.

Cross-reference by all these devices is not the only means by which a text is given coherence, a secure continuity. And progression: for, as well as ensuring smooth and coherent linearity, a text must fulfil its basic objective of moving from the position of shared knowledge and belief to the instillation of new knowledge and belief. This means clear guidance in transition from one point to the next in the discourse.

In the Simons article, the shared position is achieved by the doctor parable. From this, a generalisation is made embracing any challenge to a person's professional ability. But Simons wants us to move from this generalisation to another special class: the business executive. This is adroitly achieved by narrowing the general class to one embracing the special instance we began with, and then linking it to the special instance on which he wishes to focus the addressee's attention: *doctors and executives* (line 7). The progress of the argument in terms of the key lexical items can be summarised as follows, the numerals referring to the line numbers:

Doctors (1) ⟶ people in general (5)
⟶ doctors and executives (7)
⟶ professionals and leaders (15)
⟶ executives (19, 24), managers (34)
⟶ top management (37, 53, 55–56)

Within this general strategy of transition there are the logical, inferential, and persuasive transitions from point to point in the exposition. It may help to see the part they play in giving the piece structural unity if we look at them in text order.

The first two sentences are linked by the conjunct *after all* (line 3), the force of which is to appeal to the reader's judgement in agreeing that the atmosphere in the surgery has not changed inexplicably but rather because the doctor's ability has been challenged. The third sentence has no formal transition marker: it straightforwardly extrapolates the doctor's reaction to that of anyone.

By making a paragraph boundary at this point (line 7), the writer seeks two objectives: that the whole of what has preceded is seen as forming a unity (thus endorsing the relationships between the sentences as discussed so far); and that what follows involves both a major transition and also one that can transcend the more parochial relationship between two neighbouring sentences. In consequence, it is no surprise that, in the first sentence of the second paragraph, reference is made in line 9 to a (metaphorical)

'second opinion' linking back to lines 1–2, while the concessive conjunct *however* (line 9) neatly relates the whole of the second paragraph to the whole of the first: we may resent second opinions *but*
soon we must all face them. This is not the whole content of the
second paragraph, however: the metaphor is explained in terms of
computer programs called 'expert systems'.

Transition to the third paragraph is by means of a rather
lengthy theme recapitulating the value of expert systems and at the
same time reinforcing the futuristic momentum: an infinitive (in
this case *to make*, line 14) has a regular propensity for inviting a
forward or speculative look. In essence, the first sentence (lines 14–16)
clearly lays out the purpose of the paragraph: the need for change
in management thinking. The next two sentences are introduced
by temporal conjuncts exploring further the need for change by
contrasting most present attitudes (*currently*, line 16) with some
present developments (*already*, line 19). Since this last is indeed a
contrast, the further and concessive conjunct *however* (line 19) is
inserted to endorse it. The paragraph ends with a sentence imply-
ing that management need have no fears that computers will usurp
them, and this sentence contains another conjunct, the reassuring
of course (line 24), a common indicator of a view shared by author
and addressee.

Since 'expert systems' were introduced in the second paragraph
and were further discussed in the third, they can themselves introduce the fourth paragraph (line 26) without need of a transition
marker. The first sentence plainly implies continuity with the pre-
ceeding paragraph but also, just as plainly, implies that we are now
at the point where these systems can be explored in greater depth.
This is the role of the three sentences from line 26 to line 37.
But that section itself embodies a transition: from basic current
design to projected future development. This is assisted by the
temporal adjunct (*in the years to come*) in line 32, but the transition
leads inexorably to the recognition that *as yet* (line 37) progress is
patchy, and this leads to the further transition indicated by the
resultative conjunct in line 38. All perfectly cohesive, logical and
continuous, but (as we suggested earlier) this development in presentation leaves stranded the highly important feature about 'fuzzy'
categories. The consequence is a paragraph, uncomfortably smacking
of afterthought (lines 46–51) and requiring the only clumsy anaphoric cross-reference in the article (*Another important feature of
expert systems*, line 46): a cross-reference of the paraphrase type, but

with no clear indication to the addressee as to exactly how the linkage is to take place, since (*important*) *feature* does not straight-forwardly paraphrase any previous nominal expression.

A further unfortunate consequence of the step-by-step pro-gression from line 32 to line 45 is that the writer seems to have been unable to impose a unity on this his longest and most important paragraph. If the material in lines 46–51 had been inserted earlier in this long paragraph (say at line 32), a paragraph with an ad-mirable unity could have suitably ended at line 38. Indeed, even as the text stands, it could be argued that a new paragraph should have been opened at this point (thus beginning 'There are, as yet, very few ...').

It is as well that in this lengthy analysis of one single short piece of writing, we have been able not only to recognise with approval the quite sophisticated steps that Simons took in organising and presenting his subject, but also to venture some suggestions on how in parts the article might have been still more successful. There are few more important tasks than organising a message so as to say all and only what we want to say: and to that end we need to develop both our linguistic and our critical faculties with the greatest acuteness and sensitivity.

Lecture Six
Seeking Co-operation

Let us begin by looking at the fictional autobiography of Jane Eyre by 'Currer Bell', published in 1847. Chapter 38, which is the last chapter of the book, begins with the arresting statement:

> Reader, I married him.

And on the next page there is a question which assumes the same author-addressee posture:

> You have not quite forgotten little Adèle, have you, reader?

In 1986 we may find it rather artificial to be addressed as 'you' and to be called 'reader' by a printed voice long since dead: perhaps even more artificial to be questioned in a situation where no response can be given. Yet a response is required of us, just as a response is required of us from those questions which (as we saw in the second lecture) begin so many discourses. That response is our *co-operation*. And there is one point I would particularly like to emphasise with reference to the quotations from *Jane Eyre*. The author clearly did not feel it sufficient to have attracted her reader's attention in the first chapter and sustained it during the next thirty-seven (as she must have done, otherwise there could be no reader to address in this way in Chapter 38). Charlotte Brontë has the good communicator's instinct that her addressee must ever be borne in mind, and regularly wooed, consulted, encouraged to co-operate, right to the very end.

That instinct has to be kept alive every time we embark on a discourse. The forms and conventions involved, of course, vary from society to society, and they change with the years. We would not now in English use the word 'reader' as a term of address — still less the phrase 'Gentle Reader' of a yet earlier era. Moreover, the conventions must vary according to the medium. Charlotte

Brontë could obviously use 'reader' only to a stranger coming across her work in print: not, for example, to a friend with whom she was having a face-to-face conversation. But the need to seek co-operation is always there, and we ignore its imperatives at our own peril.

Let us pause a moment to remind ourselves first of all about the range of media in which any of us is likely to be involved — either as initiator or as receiver of discourse. It is commonplace to say there are just two: speaking and writing. But important as this distinction is, and also fundamental, it intersects with another that is also important and in some respects also fundamental: whether the addressee is an individual and known, or is general and unknown. We can illustrate these intersecting dimensions with familiar categories, as in Fig. 7.

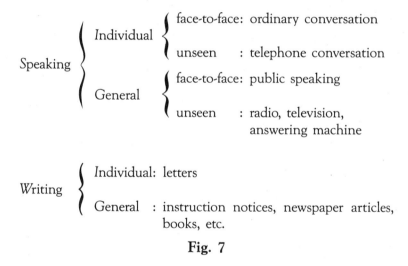

Fig. 7

It may be of interest to consider briefly an invented example from three of these possibilities:

(1) SI (face-to-face):
Well, I'm sure you sèe, don't you, Phýllis, this distínction I've been rabbiting on about between intrátextual and intértextual?

(2) SG (face-to-face):
You have been very pátient with me, ladies and géntlemen, and I hope I've expressed myself cléarly enough on the distinction I've been trying to make

between intrătextual and intèrtextual.

(3) WG (book):
A few moments' reflection — and perhaps a glance back at the examples — will no doubt be sufficient to make the reader entirely confident about the distinction drawn here between 'intratextual' and 'intertextual'.

These three examples are obviously variants of a single text with a single purpose: to stress the importance of the addressee's understanding of a terminological distinction. But they have more than this in common: they woo the addressee's co-operation and they do this in two ways. They highly esteem the addressee's role in the communication and they are relatively disparaging about the speaker/writer.

But linguistically, both these modes of wooing are very differently realised in the three examples. In the last they are most muted. Praise of the addressee is conveyed largely by implication: the writer has 'no doubt' about the addressees' ability to grasp the distinction, though careful to hint that they may need time and that it may be useful to review the examples. Disparagement of the writer is also totally oblique: largely by omission of his part in the communication (through the use of the passive participle, 'drawn') but also by hinting that the distinction is a simple ad-hoc one: the little locative adverb 'here' implies that the reader will not have come across it before because no one has previously felt it necessary to spell it out. All the same, muted or not, the readers are left in no doubt that an effort of co-operation is required of them: the more insistent perhaps, by the very confidence that the writer clearly has in their propensity to do so.

With (2), we find praise of the addressees (their plurality is made explicit) actually enveloped in the modest disparagement of the originator: in this case obviously someone speaking in some such role as lecturer. The listeners have had to exert patience, not because of the strain on their capacity to understand but because of the lecturer's lack of capacity to express himself concisely and clearly. Their co-operation is urged through being told that they are patient, by the appealing 'direct address' to them as 'you' and as 'ladies **and** gentlemen', and by the repeated use of the *I*-pronoun: not, we **notice**, the almighty 'I' of pompous authority; rather the confessional 'I' of apology: 'I *hope* I've expressed myself clearly enough', 'the distinction I've been *trying* to make'.

The appeal for co-operation by these means is brought out still more sharply in (1), beginning as it does with the invitation to 'share' conveyed by *well* (cf Svartvik, 1980). The addressee is given her personal name and the whole sentence is expressed as a question, partly by the tag 'don't you' and partly by the interrogative intonation at several nuclear points. Praise of the addressee's ability to follow is expressed by the speaker being 'sure' she sees the distinction (though this may have been overdone, leaving the addressee in a slightly awkward position if she needs to confess that she has *not* fully understood). The speaker's wry self-abasement is conveyed by the disparaging colloquialism for tedious verbosity: 'rabbiting on'.

The three samples are polar extremes in situation and style alike. In (1), the use of the singular name makes it clear that this is imagined as a situation in which two people are talking: two people, moreover, who know each other well enough to be on first-name terms and whose shared knowledge of each other is relatively great. It is thus possible for the speaker to make fairly confident assumptions and to take fairly drastic short-cuts. The degree of short-cut in the literal sense is indicated by the fact that (1) is by far the shortest of the three texts. It has only about thirty syllables, as compared with more than forty-five in (2) and around fifty-five in (3). And I choose syllables as an index of length rather than a simple word-count because it is the considerable difference in the syllable count that correlates more with the difference in style: it is not so much that there are more words in (2) and (3) as that they are *longer* and more *formal* words; less 'user-friendly' words.

Besides general brevity and the colloquial 'rabbiting', there are other indications of a relaxed approach in (1). The zero-constructed noun clause ('I'm sure you see' rather than 'I'm sure that you see') and the interpolated tag question: interpolated moreover between the verb ('see') and the object ('this distinction ...'). The speaker in fact enacts in his language the confidence in his addressee that he makes explicit in 'sure'. As well he might. The invitation to share experience by informal talk between intimates in small numbers is the commonest discourse situation that exists: something in which we are practised and adept from early childhood, though the warmth and friendliness engendered by a speaker's modesty about himself and immodesty about the addressee does not always appear to come as naturally as one might wish. Mutual involvement of speaker and hearer is in any case achieved by a multiplicity of means, not necessarily linguistic at all. In face-to-face talk, we have eye-contact, facial expressions such as appreciative smile or sympathetic frown, a head shake, shoulder movement, hand flutter: all of these invite the co-operation of the addressee or express it to the speaker — even without oral endorsement. An unmoving addressee with expressionless face is unnerving to the speaker and such behaviour is quickly taken to be a sign that co-operation is not established or has broken down. Equally, an expressionless monologue by a speaker with eyes fixed at an angle away from the addressee's face will speedily result in just such a break-down in co-operation. There are further factors, too, such as affect participants from different cultures, and there are complications (to which we are *not* inured from early childhood) involved in differences of sex, age, and hierarchical status.

But conversation need not be face-to-face: the addressee may be driving a car with the speaker sitting behind: or they may be talking in the dark as on an evening walk. Or they may be talking on the telephone. In all these situations the silent visual markers like smile or frown have to be replaced or still further endorsed by audible sounds: tag questions, interrogative interjections, or comment clauses by the speaker (*eg you see?, isn't it?, hm?, you know, I wonder, I think, I suppose*); comment clauses, agreement adverbs, or attention interjections by the addressee (*eg I do, it is, yes, really? no, hm*). Even a silence of a second or so on the telephone, and one or other participant is speedily seeking explicit co-operation: 'Are you still there?' or 'You disapprove?'.

One vitally important way of seeking or confirming co-operation is by 'turn-taking'. Monologues are unsatisfactory to both parties in conversation. Example (1) was not a rhetorical question: Phyllis was required to take her turn — if only to the extent of responding with a reassuring 'Of course'. Perhaps, in view of the speaker's use of the addressee's name, 'Of course, Tony'.

In this matter of vocatives, however, we have an aspect of discourse which is fraught with difficulty. To begin with, people vary enormously — both as individuals and as members of social groups — in the extent to which vocatives of any kind are felt necessary or desirable. If everyone recognised this (that some people like to keep using their addressee's name as they speak while others do not), one problem would disappear. But some people feel a speaker is too gushy or intrusive if their name keeps being introduced, while others feel a speaker is cold or distant if their name never occurs.

Another problem is that people are often uncertain as to the appropriate vocative for the relationship that exists between speaker and addressee. It is well-known that Americans in general proceed from title plus surname (*Mrs Wong*) to first name (*Mary*) more quickly than the British in general do. But the rate of progress is affected by sex and sex mix (man to man; man to woman; woman to woman; and certainly slowest of all, woman to man). It is affected by age (young person to young person; the older to a younger person; and certainly slowest of all, younger person to a decidedly older one). And of course it is affected too by hierarchy in an organisation. Then again, there is the range and use of vocatives that do not involve personal names at all: *Doctor, Vice-Chancellor, Minister, Your Excellency, Mr Dean, Sergeant,*[1] *Sir, Madam*, at one extreme (the last two illustrate an area in which English is widely felt to be deficient); *old man, darling, my dear, mate, chum, love*, etc, at the other extreme. All this I must leave totally out of account, as also hypocoristics like *Charlie* beside *Charles*. I must ignore too the effect of switches 'up' rather than 'down' the formality scale. A boy who is used to being called *Tony* by his parents or teacher will freeze on hearing 'Anthony, where were you last night?'.

With sample (2), we confront problems of an entirely different order, since we are no longer dealing with a discourse situation for which we are all trained by straightforward life-long experience. There are conventions to be learned and techniques of group dynamics to be acquired — usually by observation of more practised public speakers and by trial-and-error experience of one's own. As presented, the sample is more likely to be heard in a room such as an auditorium with speaker and audience able to see each other. The vocative 'ladies and gentlemen' would be unusual in an address to an unseen audience — as in radio or television. And it also requires a certain critical mass: it would sound more than a little odd so to address a minimum plurality (say two women and two men). But the wording of (2) implies a very large gathering — more than fifty or sixty people, let us say — because the practised speaker's use

---

[1]In military discourse, vocatives are often obligatory:
    A: How long have you been in the army, corporal?
    B: Just over a year.
    A: Just over a year, *sir*, — as you ought to know by now.

of eye-contact and audience reaction would otherwise give him the answer to his implied question. A good teacher, for example, can usually tell by glancing round his class of twenty or even thirty students whether a point he has made has been adequately understood.

Ensuring such co-operation with radio and television audiences is more difficult but one useful and widely practised device is the so-called studio audience. This works in two ways. The feedback from the physically present audience assures the speaker that he or she is carrying that group along at an appropriate rate (not too fast to lose some and not too slow so as to bore others). One is thus able to treat the studio audience as a sample of the indefinitely large audience listening or viewing at home. At the same time, sitting at home (even alone) we are thereby helped to feel part of the communication process by being able in some sense to identify with members of the studio audience whose reactions we can see or hear. If they can understand, we say, then so can we. If the studio audience responds appreciatively to a witticism, we at home feel encouraged to do likewise.

But of course most radio and television discourse is without the support of a studio audience, and in these circumstances the conventions are usually very different. Although the broadcaster may be addressing an audience totalling hundreds of thousands, a producer may insist that the posture be that of a one-to-one communication with the assumption of the solo viewer or listener, alone in a private room, as the type of audience as a whole. This is why 'ladies and gentlemen' is regarded as inappropriate as a vocative, and broadcasting convention (in the English-speaking world at least) provides no singular substitute: there is no radio or television analogue to the 'Reader, I married him' of *Jane Eyre*. Subject pronouns can be *you*, but in a singular sense: thus 'You can work this out for yourself', rather than 'You can work this out for *yourselves*'.

It is of considerable interest to observe the way in which teachers in Open University programmes adopt (or adapt) the language of the private tutorial rather than the lecture theatre. Through the courtesy of Dr John Coyle of the Open University's Chemistry Department, I am able to quote from the script he used in his very interesting television programme on chemical reactions which I watched in June 1985:

I don't suppose it would take you long to suggest a

reason for these[1] different stereo-chemical results, but what about the reaction mechanisms to explain the results?

We should note the attempt at a direct speaker-addressee relationship between 'I' and 'you'; the encouragement of the addressee's ability and the encouragement also to *co-operation*. The first part of the sentence stimulates the addressee to formulate an explanation of phenomena just presented, though of course the invitation to 'suggest' a reason is pure convention: there can be no real turn-taking. The speaker cannot hear the suggestion he is evoking (though the enacting of a turn-taking situation is often incorporated in distance-educational work by periodic short silences in which the addressee is encouraged to respond orally or in imagination, in the solitary privacy of his home). In the second part of the quotation, there is a question: but it is not a question requiring the addressee to think of an answer. It is one of those presentational questions we considered in the second lecture: a scene-setting for what follows. Such a question tells the addressee that the speaker will in fact be answering it; and that is precisely what Dr Coyle went on to do.

Mention has already been made of the bonding function of *I* and *you* in discourse, but there is one other pronoun which strongly endorses the search for co-operation in communication, and that is *we*. In large measure, of course, this is the corollary of *I* and *you*: the so-called 'inclusive' *we*, as in

I would like to ask *you* if *we* might discuss something.

Here *we* stands for both speaker and addressee. A very common use of the first-person plural to invite discoursal co-operation is the objective form *us* in the *let's* construction. In the Open University chemistry transmission, there were numerous instances; for example:

Now let's apply these stereo-chemicals criteria to the two cyclo-addition reactions you saw earlier in the programme.

A further illustration, this time one in which the subject form *we*

---

[1]Here, and in the examples to follow, the deictics such as *these* and verbs such as *look* relate to sophisticated visual accompaniments including coloured models with movable parts.

occurs just before the objective *us*:

> Now we want to relate these geometrical isomers to ways
> in which two butene molecules can come together con-
> certedly. Let's look first at the cis, cis, cis isomer.

Just as the *let's* construction is often called the 'first-person imperative', so the effect of *we* in the first line of this example is a gentle
bullying of the addressee to join the speaker in wanting to do
something. The consequence is that in much discourse of an in-
structional or persuasive kind, *we* can be regarded as a politely
conventional equivalent of *I* — since of course it is *I*, the speaker,
who decides what is wanted and what is next to be explored. But
equally, *we* can be regarded as equivalent to *you*, since it is the
addressee that the speaker is seeking to instruct or persuade. Yet
notice the very considerable difference in effect between such sets
as the following:

1(a) So let's now look at a pericyclic reaction.
 (b) I shall now show you a pericyclic reaction.
 (c) You will now see a pericyclic reaction.

2(a) Now we want to relate these geometrical isomers
      to ways in which two butene molecules can come
      together concertedly.
 (b) Now I'd like to relate these geometrical isomers to
      ways in which two butene molecules can come
      together concertedly.
 (c) Now you should relate these geometrical isomers
      to ways in which two butene molecules can come
      together concertedly.

3(a) Here we have the trans trans isomer of the diene.
 (b) Here I show the trans trans isomer of the diene.
 (c) Here you have the trans trans isomer of the diene.

The (a) item in each case is Dr Coyle's version, and we can readily
appreciate how much more effective it is in achieving the student's
co-operation by the assumption of an inclusive team effort — in
contrast to the guru-like remoteness of 'I' in the (b) set or the way
in which the addressee is equally isolated in the (c) set.

But there is a further use of *we* in discourse which contributes to addressee involvement, though in fact it less resembles the
inclusive *we* already discussed than an exclusive *we* that I have

not so far mentioned. This is illustrated by the italicised pronouns in the following:

> Jill and I have finished the job *we*'ve been doing, Mr Lee; have you anything else you'd like *us* to do?

Here, obviously, *we* and *us* exclude the addressee. In this light, it is worth considering the following example from Dr Coyle's chemistry programme:

> Now since both of these rotations occur simultaneously, there are two possible combinations. Either both are clockwise or anti-clockwise (we call that *conrotatory* reaction). Or the rotations occur in opposite senses: one clockwise and one anti-clockwise (that we call *disrotatory* reaction).

Unlike Coyle's use of *we* that I said earlier could be replaced by *I* or *you*, this *we* more resembles a pronoun with third-person reference, as if Coyle had said '*scientists* call this "conrotatory"'. But that would have seemed to exclude both speaker and addressee from the statement, while '*we* scientists call this "conrotatory"' would have seemed to exclude the addressee and rather pompously align the speaker with the sources of authority. By using *we* in a context where replacement by 'you and I' would be absurd, Coyle nonetheless implies that, since his use of *we* normally includes the addressee, the student here too is invited to join the experts in adopting the terminology explained, so that hereafter *we* can indeed mean 'you and I'.

We can now return to the three samples with which this lecture began (and in thus expressing myself, I am aware that the sensitised reader may now be deflected from the content to the expression: my use of *we* and my choice of 'with which this lecture began' in preference to alternatives such as 'with which I began this lecture'). The third sample represented *written* communication: more specifically, *printed* communication, since its form is such as to make it clear that no specific individual is being addressed, as would be the case in a hand-written or typed *letter*:

> A few moments' reflection — and perhaps a glance back at the examples — will no doubt be sufficient to make the reader entirely confident about the distinction drawn here between 'intratextual' and 'intertextual'.

In the light of the foregoing discussion, the contrast between this
and the other two samples is striking in the absence of both *I* and
you. The writer lurks in the background, as it were, and does not
obtrude; the addressee is referred to with a third-person phrase,
'the reader', rather than being directly addressed. Although this
example is by no means extreme in assuming such a detached
posture (the tone is in fact fairly warm and informal), many writers
prefer to declare their own personal involvement more explicitly as
well as their direct relationship with their readers. And as in the
Charlotte Brontë example, just as radio and television audiences
are not addressed collectively, such writers would treat readers as
singular, as individuals. Thus in a book on typography, it would
not be unusual to find a presentation of the following kind:

> If you now examine your own copy of this book, you
> will see how I have juxtaposed roman and italic type
> of the same font but have avoided the use of bold-face
> type except for headings.

In other words, the co-operation-seeking mechanisms of speech
are often mirrored as closely as possible in printed discourse; and
reference to the addressee as 'the reader', to the author as 'the writer'
(or as 'we'), or the avoidance of reference to either (as by the use
of the passive) will tend to be regarded as too distant and formal,
even for print. Contrast:

> If a copy of the present book is examined, it will be
> seen that roman and italic type of the same font can
> be found in juxtaposition ...

So it is that, although we must expect to find page after page
in a book or newspaper without mention of author or addressee,
the tenor of written communication has generally come to reflect
in recent years a re-awakening of the traditional instincts for seeking the close co-operation of those to whom a communication is
addressed. This is natural enough where it is plainly in the communicator's personal interest to achieve the addressee's co-operation:
as in advertising. Natural enough, too, in an educational climate
in which students are persuaded and encouraged to learn, rather
than one in which they are obliged to do so by *force majeure*; the
pedagogical style of text books and teachers has changed out of
all recognition in my life time. (Cf Sinclair and Brazil, 1982.)
    It is less natural in the discoursal posture of civil, military, and

legal authority, where various factors (such as an authoritative tradition, the overriding need for precision, and the importance of ensuring compliance rather than just voluntary co-operation) combine to take the addressee's ability and willingness to co-operate somewhat for granted. Consider the following not atypical quotation from an insurance policy:

> If the Insured submits to the [name] Insurance Company a written proposal which, it is hereby agreed, shall be the basis of this contract, and if the particulars therein set forth are accurate, and if the Insured pays to the Company the premium for insurance, the Company will indemnify the Insured by payment ...

Few of us would expect a legal contract to adopt a chatty style like 'Well, if you do this, I will do that'. But there is a world of difference between such informal use of the language normally associated with co-operation and the chill distance between writer and addressee found in this document. In consequence, there has been something of a consumer revolt during the past decade, with 'Plain English' movements growing increasingly active in the United States, Britain, and in Australia. It is interesting, in fact, that the problem has thus been diagnosed in terms of the tortuous complexity of the language found in official documents — the hard, 'user-*un*friendly' words, the long clauses, the forbidding array of negatives and conditionals — rather than in terms of the human relations between writer and addressee, company and client, government and citizen. In contrast to the earlier efforts by Sir Ernest Gowers and others in the United Kingdom to *encourage* civil servants to use 'plain words' in their documents (and corresponding moves in America to remove 'gobbledegook' from official pronouncements), the Plain English Law passed by the New York Legislature in November 1978 *required* all consumer agreements to be written in 'a clear and coherent manner using words with common and everyday meanings'. In 1979 President Carter issued an Executive Order, analogously phrased and motivated. In 1982, the British Government (responding, in part, to pressure from the National Consumer Council) issued a White Paper entitled *Administrative Forms in Government*, directing departments to design forms in keeping with the principles of the Plain English movement. And in 1984 the Australian Government launched an official campaign with similar goals.

But while the focus of all these developments is explicitly on the 'plainness' and simplicity of expression, the effect is to design documents facilitating the co-operation of the addressee along lines discussed in the present lecture. Thus among the trial documents being evaluated this year in Australia is an application form for car registration. Here is an extract:

> Please do your best to fill in this form. If you have problems, ask the Motor Registration Office. Our address and telephone are at the end of this form.
>
> Start with Part 1 'About the owner'. Go slowly and carefully. Only miss out questions when the form tells you to.

Author (*we*: 'Our address ...') and addressee are identified (*you* is used repeatedly); some sense of co-operation between the two is implied by distancing both from the form (which is the source of any 'problems' and which 'tells you' to do things; *we*, by contrast, help *you*).

I have said nothing about the role of other devices such as rhetorical questions, but it is needless to point out that there are many more points involved in 'seeking co-operation' than it is possible to cover in a single lecture. There is for example (to name just one) the formulation that has been called 'the pragmatic conditional' (cf Haegeman, 1984). We have already noted the use of conditional clauses as politely disguised imperatives. Thus the example beginning 'If you now examine your own copy' comes close to meaning 'Now examine your own copy'. Nonetheless, the conditional here is logically normal: 'If x, then y', thus permitting the inference 'If not x, then not y': 'If you don't examine your copy, you won't see my use of roman and italic'.

The pragmatic conditional is different in having no such logical relation with the rest of the sentence. For example:

> If you remember, I introduced in my first lecture a distinction between 'intratextual' and 'intertextual'.

Clearly, I made the distinction whether or not you remember my doing so and by the same token, there can in this case be no negative analogue:

> If you don't remember, I didn't introduce in my first lecture a distinction between 'intratextual' and 'intertextual'.

But equally clearly, the role of the pragmatic conditional is communicatively similar to the role of the logical conditional that I exemplified earlier. 'If you now examine your own copy' and 'If you remember' both function as directives to the addressee: 'Please co-operate by examining your own copy', '... by remembering the distinction I introduced'.

Pragmatic conditionals help the co-operation process in other ways too. They can soften an interruptive correction:

> If I can just break in there, President Kennedy was assassinated in Dallas, not in Houston.

They allow apologetic reinforcement of a terminological point:

> The child's *competence* is not in question, if you'll permit that Chomskyan concept.

They can nudge the addressee into recognising an allusion, at the same time enabling the speaker to seem disarmingly modest:

> Hilton hotels are scattered right throughout this dark world and wide — if I've got the Miltonic phrase right.

The various kinds of tactful invitation to co-operate that we have been exploring in this lecture are not an absolute *necessity* in communication. Their use (like their frequency) depends on our intuitions about the extent to which it is necessary to engage (or re-engage) our addressee's willing attention. When we embark on discourse, we can usually be confident that the addressee is predisposed to believe what we are saying or writing; is ready to find our discourse of relevance — ready indeed to seek out such relevance if it is not immediately apparent. In short, our addressee is keen to co-operate. But we should not be so careless of our addressee's interest as to take all this for granted. Nor would it be in our own interest to do so. By the cultivation of modesty on the communicator's part and by offering encouragement and help to our addressee, we help ourselves in turn by keeping our antennae sensitively alert to the danger of being only partially understood. And we often learn more of what we mean ourselves.

Lecture Seven
A Sense of the Appropriate

The subject of the present lecture does not mean that I have ignored until such a late point in this series the need to make the language of every discourse appropriate to the occasion. In Lecture Three, there was occasion to quote Thumboo on the need 'to maintain decorum between a subject and its mode of expression'. The whole purpose of Lecture Six, moreover, was to insist that in seeking the co-operation of our addressee, we simultaneously seek modes of expression appropriate to the medium and the nature of the communication. And we looked at one text, the quotation from an insurance policy, where it was clear that the writer's concept of what was linguistically necessary and fitting militated sharply against the criterion of seeking co-operation. I would like now to go on and explore more broadly the effects of taste, convention, subject matter, occasion and other factors upon the selection of words and grammar.

There was an occasion when Charles Dickens was guest at dinner with two artist friends. He was so pleased with the food that he asked if the cook could be summoned 'and I will address her in appropriate language'. 'No doubt you would', replied his host. 'But like most cooks, she has uncertain temper ... She wouldn't understand your "appropriate language" as meant seriously, and she might resent it in her own language, which I believe, is sometimes described ... as "bad language".' So, even on a specific occasion, two people may have sharply different views on what is appropriate.

Many present-day popular writers have developed a remarkable flair for exploiting the range of linguistic repertoire thought essential for specific occasions. An example is the American Michael M. Thomas, whose novel *Green Monday* (1980) shows keen interest in the smart language affected by modern executives. At one point, a Minister of a developing country was heard to say 'it makes sense for us to expand, materially, our position in common stocks, for which we can foresee a significantly improved environment'. In consequence, a character proceeded to comment on the 'pompous, synthetic vocabulary' and to wonder where on earth people 'learn to talk that way'. A sardonic answer was at once provided. 'It was called Business English, was taught in business schools, and has developed to confer a quality of intellectual and philosophical legitimacy on the otherwise simple, vulgar matter of buying and selling things'. And a little later we read:

> Nyquist had been early to recognise that the creative coinage of buzzwords and professional argot had come to be ... important in the investment business ...
>
> 'No problem', said Nyquist kindly. 'These days the number of new M.D.s[1] gets pretty confusing. What order of magnitude are we talking about?'
>
> 'Well, our going-in increments add up to three-quarter K square.'
>
> 'That is a very substantial GII, Mr Axelson.'
>
> 'It's a number of large accounts shifting transients' ...
>
> 'Absolute *value wise* — AVW, as we call it — you're reaching beyond our current on-shelf capability. How do you see this working out?'
>
> Harrison pulled out the plan ... He had revised its language thoroughly. This was the part he had rehearsed for two weeks. He was reminded of Hamlet's instruction to the players: speak the gobbledygook trippingly.
>
> 'Well', he said, handing Nyquist the folder, 'this is all in layman's language. I just don't have a handle yet on all the tangential percipients that go into a high-arc MPL-type matrix. Obviously, for these magnitude gradients we'll need a broadwash diversification — spectrumwise, that is. I've suggested a four-digit context ...'

This is not 'in layman's language', of course, and the allusion to Hamlet is appropriate. Harrison ('Mr Axelson') is trying to beat Nyquist at his own game and is ready to overstate, if anything, his ability to use the appropriate jargon.

There are other occasions when it is better to affect the converse and to protest a reluctance, even inability, to use impressive language. In a love poem called 'Apology for Understatement',

---

[1]Module designations.

John Wain writes:

> Forgive me that I pitch your praise too low.
> Such reticence my reverence demands,
> For silence falls with laying on of hands.
>
> Forgive me that my words come thin and slow.
> This could not be a time for eloquence,
> For silence falls with healing of the sense.
>
> We only utter what we lightly know,
> And it is rather that my love knows me.
> It is that your perfection set me free.
>
> Verse is dressed up that has nowhere to go.
> You took away my glibness with my fear.
> Forgive me that I stand in silence here.
>
> It is not words could pay you what I owe.

The 'I' in this poem is no less disingenuous, we must note, than Thomas' character Harrison with his nonchalant claim to be speaking 'in layman's language'. The lover's words do not 'come thin and slow': they are rich in their vibrancy and have obviously been chosen with meticulous care. But the point Wain makes is *not* disingenuous, any more than is the point made in the book by Michael Thomas. There is an indefinitely wide range of occasions and there is a need to fit to each a linguistic style that is appropriate. Everyone 'in his time plays many parts', and our communicative education consists in large measure of learning our lines. We talk to our children with words and even grammar we would not dream of using to adult members of the family; a father may address his three-year-old daughter, for example, like this:

> Daddy's a weeny bit too tired to play with his Jenny-
> kins tonight, poppet.

Baby words, you notice, such as *weeny* and possibly *Daddy*; hypocoristics like *Jennykins*; vocatives like *poppet*; grammar such as third-person forms replacing *I* and *you*.

We speak to a visitor in our office in a different style from the one we adopt in speaking to a colleague in the same office. We write a letter applying to a stranger for a job in very different language

from that used in a letter to a friend. These are among the common parts that virtually everyone 'in his time plays'. Yet even with
one or two of these, we may feel hesitant about going on stage (if
I may persist in the Jacques metaphor): how to sound formal and
courteous enough to the stranger who walks into your office —
without seeming to be too starchy on the one hand, too servile
on the other. But at least in this situation you can play it by ear
and eye, adjusting your style to the way your visitor responds.
Writing to a stranger for a job, or with a suggestion, or with a
request for information is another matter. You can't play it by ear
in this case: you have little chance of ever knowing the impression
your letter gave of you and of your sense of appropriacy.

And these, I say again, are discoursal situations that are
commonplace. But in this contracting world of faster travel and
ever-extending channels of communication, more and more of us
are involved in discourse that takes us outside our local compound;
more and more of us are using an international language which
is not our native tongue. And the more successful we are in our
careers, the more varieties of appropriate language we have to master
(not to mention the obvious obverse: the more varieties of appropriate language we master, the more successful we are likely to be
in our careers). Needless to say in Singapore of all countries, the
international use of English (in a world where most languages still
keep to their familiar and traditional *intra*national functions) has
accentuated the problem of matching purpose with appropriacy.
How do you write to the American head office of a multinational
corporation? How do you open negotiation with the Ministry of
Trade in Tokyo? It may even fall to our lot to write the text for
a ceremonial plaque or for an illuminated address to some retiring
dignitary.

On admission to the profession as veterinary surgeons in
the UK, all the new graduates stand and make a choric declaration
as follows:

> Inasmuch as the privilege of Membership of the Royal
> College of Veterinary Surgeons is about to be conferred
> on me, I promise and solemnly declare that I will abide
> in all due loyalty to the Royal College of Veterinary
> Surgeons and will do all in my power to maintain and
> promote its interests. I further promise that I will pursue
> the work of my profession with uprightness of conduct

> and that my constant endeavour will be to ensure the welfare of animals committed to my care.

At this point, while the graduates remain standing, the President addresses them in similarly rotund terms:

> In the name of the Council of the Royal College of Veterinary Surgeons and by virtue of the power conferred upon them by Royal Charter and by Act of Parliament, I do hereby admit you as members of the Royal College and by the same power do confer upon you the right to be styled Veterinary Surgeons and to be known and deemed and recognised henceforth as duly qualified members of the veterinary profession.

Words of power! 'I ... do confer upon you ...'

When, as Vice-Chancellor in London, I was first privileged to attend this ceremony and hear a cohort of young vet graduates take their oath and receive their admission, I was struck by the solemnity and seriousness which the language helped to confer on the occasion, and I was particularly struck by the unfamiliarity of it. Indeed, some of the language (*eg* 'I will abide ... to the ... College') was quite beyond my own experience. I assumed it was hallowed by age, and so I made inquiries. To my surprise, I found that it had been specifically written only about a generation ago: to be precise, in 1959. In other words, the language of this ceremony is in one sense contemporary: yet in another sense, its roots are long and deep in the tradition of solemn rhetoric. That tradition permits, if not enjoins, such features as the use of *do* in verb phrases ('I do hereby admit you') where in general English it occurs only in negative and interrogative clauses. We note also the co-ordinating of verbs complementary in meaning: *promise and ... declare*; *maintain and promote*; *to be known and deemed and recognised*. Above all, we note the tone of ritual associated with performative verbal behaviour, especially the vicarious verbal behaviour as we have it here: 'in the name of the Council ... I do hereby admit you' (cf Searle, 1979). Although there are a few common performative verbs for a few common occasions, and although even vicarious performatives can occur without due ceremony (as in 'I thank you most sincerely on behalf of the whole team'), the act of 'doing things with words' — as opposed to using words to *describe* things — is generally accompanied by a special sense of occasion. There is marriage, for example, or making one's will, or naming a child. In most societies, these occasions seem to call for memorable language to match the solemnity of commitment: and as we want to emphasise the permanence of commitment, it seems appropriate to replicate the forms of language used in other such declarations. Inevitably this means archaic language, as though we were declaring a continuing renewal of respected procedures. Let me give an extreme example of this in the language used for formal purposes by the British Crown — extreme in its historic vibrance but readily paralleled in the analogous linguistic rituals of far younger English-speaking countries.

The excerpts that follow are from the charter granted to a constituent College within the federal University of London as recently as 1980:

> Elizabeth the Second
> by the Grace of God of the United Kingdom of Great Britain and Northern Ireland and of Our other Realms and Territories Queen, Head of the Commonwealth, Defender of the Faith:
>
> TO ALL TO WHOM THESE PRESENTS SHALL COME, GREETING!
>
> WHEREAS an humble Petition has been presented unto Us by Our most dearly beloved Mother, Queen Elizabeth the Queen Mother, Chancellor of Our University of London ... praying that We should be graciously pleased to grant a Charter to King's College London ...
>
> NOW THEREFORE KNOW YE that We by virtue of Our Prerogative Royal and of Our especial grace, certain knowledge and mere motion have willed and ordained and by these Presents do for Us, Our Heirs and Successors will and ordain as follows:
>
> 1. In this Our Charter ...
>
> [numbered clauses follow]
>
> 19. Our Royal Will and Pleasure is that this Our Charter shall ever be construed benevolently and in every case

most favourably to the College and to the promotion
of the objects of this Our Charter.

IN WITNESS whereof We have caused these Our Letters to be made Patent.

WITNESS Ourself at Westminster the 28th day of
January in the twenty-seventh year of Our Reign.

BY WARRANT UNDER THE QUEEN'S SIGN
MANUAL

Numerous features here are at once recognisable as totally exotic
to ordinary English usage. There is the royal *We*, its uniqueness
of reference symbolised by an initial capital and its singular reference
indicated by the emphatic *Ourself* being singular in form. There
are the French grammatical calques, as in the postposed adjective
manual in the *Queen's sign manual*. The whole text deserves careful
study not only in its own right and in the bearing it has upon
the special language of all legal documents, but also because —
extreme though it is — this text illustrates so unambiguously the
fundamental principles of appropriacy in language.

Perhaps most important among these is conformity with expectation. The words 'I am somewhat tired, Jennifer' can only in
a rather superficial sense be thought equivalent to 'Daddy's a weeny
bit tired, Jennykins': to the little girl herself they could certainly
not be regarded as equal alternatives and the former might even
make her fear that her father had stopped loving her.

There are certain varieties of presentational style where conformity with expectation is matched by the communicative efficiency
of the linguistic forms. This I believe to be true for most uses of
the passive found in conventional scientific description. From a
literary point of view, it may sound stilted (and from a human point
of view, coldly impersonal), but when we read some such sentence
as 'Temperature and viscosity measures were recorded every six
hours', it is surely more satisfactory than any active-voice alternative
could be. We do not want to know who recorded the measures —
and, quite apart from the clumsiness, it would have been difficult for
the author to try and tell us, since it could obviously not have been
the same person on more than two successive occasions — if that.

There is a similar justification in efficiency for the easily
recognisable style of recipes. First a list of requisite ingredients;

then a sequence of imperative sentences which (conveniently for the reader) gives the order of operations:

> Heat oil in a kwali and stir-fry the onion, garlic, ginger and chillies over a low fire till fragrant but not brown.
>
> Add the pork and prawns, and stir-fry for a minute before putting in sugar and the oyster, light and dark soya sauces.
>
> When the meat is cooked and fragrant, mash the *doufu* in with the meat. Mix well.
>
> Add the beaten egg and stir for a minute or two before removing the kwali from the fire. Stir in the coriander leaves and serve hot with rice or bread.
>
> (*The Sunday Times*, Singapore, 8 December 1985)

But for the most part, appropriacy and conformity with expectation have little to do with making the communication readily and efficiently assimilable. In some cases, as with the stately language of royal charters, they actually work *against* easy understanding. To a less dramatic extent, the same is probably true for some of the most familiar occasion-bound styles of English. Thus what is obviously regarded as appropriate in journalism does not seem to have among its criteria ease and speed of comprehension. Let me just quote two examples from different sections of the same day's paper (the precise reference given is in fact irrelevant, since this presentational style occurs in the daily press throughout the English-speaking world):

> (1) Actor Fred Grandy, who has played television's Love Boat purser, Burl 'Gopher' Smith, for nine years, announced yesterday he will abandon ship to run for Congress in land-locked Iowa.
>
> (2) Stefan Edberg toppled world No. 1 Ivan Lendl to-day to make the men's singles final of the Australian Open tennis championships.
>
> Edberg outlasted the top-seeded Czech in a mara-thon five-setter to join defending champion Mats Wilander in the Final — the first between two Swedes in a Grand Slam event.
>
> The 19-year-old right-hander won 6–7, 3–7, 7–5, 6–1, 9–7 in a match lasting just over four hours.
>
> (*Straits Times*, 9 December 1985)

In having heavy and lengthy subjects such as that in (1), and in
having extensive premodification in noun-phrase structure (as in
The 19-year-old right-hander), this type of writing subverts some of
the desiderata for information-processing which — as we saw in
Lecture Five — speeds the addressee's understanding. Yet these and
other features satisfy criteria of appropriacy in press reportage,
doubtless through the impression of compactness that they convey.
In 'Edberg outlasted the top-seeded Czech', the writer contrives to
tell us that Lendl is Czech and that he had been 'seeded' number
one. Not so much *tell* us perhaps as *remind* us, since a striking
feature of press style is to treat as though 'given' a good deal of
information that may in fact be 'new' to us, pretending to assume
in us far more sophistication and knowledge than we have. A sense
of smart neatness may also be the justification for the use of resultative infinitive clauses. But '*to make*' the final, '*to join* Wilander'
are in fact little shorter than 'and so made', 'and so joins', and a
more plausible objective is simply to observe the conventions of
press style.

   If we take a form of discourse less extreme in style than either
royal charters or daily newspapers, we find nonetheless that appropriacy resides more in convention than in rapidity of assimilation.
The following example will strike anyone engaged in literary studies
as perfectly normal; plain rather than high flown, simple and direct
rather than obscure and complicated:

> Melchiori, in an intricate study of the poem, showed
> that *Sailing to Byzantium* recalls Yeats's earlier story,
> *Rosa Alchemica*, and so there is no reason to doubt
> that the poem is a finished version of Yeats's kind of
> alchemical quest. The highest claim yet made for *Sailing
> to Byzantium* is that of Whitaker, who says of this poem
> and *Among School Children* that 'in them is created a
> new species of man who — unbeknownst to himself,
> as it were — *is* his contrary.' Yeats would have delighted
> in this claim, but that the poem justifies it is open
> to question.
>   (Harold Bloom, *Yeats*, New York: OUP, 1970)

Yet compared with the way the same critic would have expressed
himself in a face-to-face tutorial, the language of the printed version
shows a deliberate distancing. Thus the cataphoric mode of referring is markedly elegant, *the poem* coming before the identification

of it by title; in less self-conscious English, we would expect:

> In a study of *Sailing to Byzantium*, Melchiori showed
> that the poem recalls ...

the noun phrase *the poem* now assuming the more usual anaphoric
mode. The double negative in 'there is no reason to doubt' would
be less likely in speech than 'there is reason to believe', with no
negative at all. The anaphoric *that* in *that of Whitaker* is again a
feature of belles-lettristic prose; in speech, Bloom would probably
have used the genitive: 'The highest claim is Whitaker's'. Finally, we
may note the noun clause as subject in the closing sentence; ease of
communication (through the principles of end-weight and end-focus
discussed in Lecture Five) would demand rather the postponement
of the noun clause and the use of *it* as anticipatory subject:

> It is open to question that [*or more usually still* whether]
> the poem justifies it.

So far, in discussing appropriacy in respect of these samples, I
have drawn attention to features of *grammar*, but it will not have
escaped notice that the selection of *lexical items* varies from text
to text in ways that are at least as striking. Differences in vocabulary, however, are occasioned in two quite distinct ways. For the
most part, lexical selection depends on subject matter. Expressions
like *straight sets* or *top-seed* concern tennis and for that reason alone
could not be expected in a statutory document. By the same token,
one would not find words like *kwali*, *stir-fry*, or *chillies* in a report
of a tennis tournament or a soccer match. On content-dependence
in vocabulary selection I shall have no more to say. But the other
determinant in preferring one word to another is style-dependence,
in other words a sense of appropriacy; and it is on this that I should
like to dwell, however briefly.

A few days ago, a companion looked up from the morning
newspaper and made a remark which I heard as:

> McEnroe is going to win.

My response was 'Win what? Where is the next international tournament?' 'No, no', was the reply. 'The paper says he's getting married';
and I was then shown the newspaper headline:

> McEnroe to Wed

I had as it were 'misheard', not because there had been any failure to enunciate the verb *wed* clearly but because this verb belongs so solidly to the language of the press (and largely to press headlines at that) as to make it totally unexpected for me to hear spoken around the breakfast table. I had therefore automatically substituted another verb of similar phonological structure carrying a far greater predictability both in terms of what I knew about McEnroe and of what I knew about informal conversation.

Important as are grammar and sentence-structure in matching language to occasion, there is no area of language comparable with vocabulary in the extent of its influence in conferring a sense of appropriacy. This comes out with startling clarity in the passage from Thomas' *Green Monday* quoted early in this lecture. Some of the words are content-determined: in the content of investment discourse, words like *account, increment,* and *diversification* will occur naturally enough. But the vast majority of the words paraded between Nyquist and Harrison are selected in order to assure each other that each is thoroughly at home in the form of jargon which certain kinds of business executive regard as appropriate to their profession. Thus we have *order of magnitude* instead of the less style-specific word *scale; a four-digit context* instead of *a four-figure number* or (less specialised still) *some thousands; on shelf* for *available;* the retreat from full words into the privacy of acronyms (*AVW* for *absolute value wise,* MD for *module designation* — though even the full versions are style-specific themselves); the use of *K* instead of *thousand.*

It scarcely needs to be said that the excerpt from Michael Thomas is not only fictional but comically marked by hyperbolic parody (cf Nash, 1985). Nonetheless, in non-fictional texts, vocabulary tends to be just as clearly indicative of the appropriate style. The text of the procedure of admission to the veterinary profession was dignified by words essentially ceremonious: *deemed* for *regarded as; henceforth* instead of *from now on; styled* for *called; confer* for *give; committed* for *put* or *placed.* In the Royal Charter, we find *petition* for *request; praying* for *asking; pleased* for *willing; ordained* for *instructed; construed* for *interpreted; patent* for *available or public;* most style-specific of all, *these presents* for *this document.*

In the second press example, there occurs the verb *toppled* for *beat.* One of the striking features of what constitutes appropriacy in sports reporting is a lively violence in the verbs: *slam, bag, slug, stump, thrash, wham, knock out, crush,* and many other

such inelegant variations. Much of this reflects a verbal playful-
ness, a self-consciousness in the selection of vocabulary, which often
aspires to a modest degree of artistry. This is notable in the first
of the two press examples. An actor called Fred Grandy has decided
to go into politics. The journalist might have seized the occasion
to capitalise on his readers' shared knowledge of the most notable
analogue that would spring to the mind of any of us: President
Reagan. The writer decides to be more original and to take as his
starting point a presumed knowledge of Grandy's television role
as a ship's purser. This becomes the springboard for the lexically
appropriate metaphor of 'abandoning ship' as Grandy turns to
politics, a metaphor which is then sustained in the otherwise irrelevant (though wittily ironic and geographically correct) description
of Iowa as being 'land-locked'.

Sustaining a metaphor (and more particularly avoiding a
mixture of metaphors) is of course a feature of all good discourse,
irrespective of the particular style. It is a special aspect of what one
might call the lexical structure of a communication. I have stressed
that a word may be appropriate to one type of discourse where it
is not appropriate to another. But this is an oversimplification. What
constitutes a sense of lexical structure is less the occurence of an
individual word than the *co*-occurence of that word with others
of the same tone. Thus the recipe which I quoted not merely has
words which individually are appropriate to cooking: they also
fittingly collocate with each other. If in place of the instruction
Mix well, the writer had put *Achieve total diffusion*, this would have
struck a lexically absurd and discordant note; yet *total diffusion* for
thorough mixing would have been lexically appropriate in certain
scientific texts — accompanied of course by analogous collocates
of the kind we would expect to find in scientific exposition.

There has been in fact an internal lexical harmony in each
of the texts we have examined: words keeping company with others
of their kind. This is supremely true of the poem by John Wain
— as we should expect, since the careful and sensitive selection of
the *mot juste* is the hallmark of poetry and other good literature.
The key words in the poem — *silence, praise, sense, perfection, elo-
quence, reticence, reverence* — are all congruently suggestive of solemn
dignity, and Wain has two reasons for choosing such words. First,
he wants to convey his gratitude to the woman for reciprocating
his love for her. Second, he seems to give this gratitude additional
force by conveying to her that the amorous experience has been
tantamount to a religious experience. This tone is heralded by the

word *praise* in the first line, but it is only when this word is replaced by *reverence* in the second line that the religious aura is
unmistakable. Whereas the word *praise* is Janus-faced or at any rate
neutral in stylistic tone (one can praise a good dinner or one can
praise almighty God), the word *reverence* belongs to religious discourse alone. Thus when we come to the third line ('silence falls
with laying on of hands'), we are ready to read this in two ways:
the adoring silence of the lover as his hands start to caress, and
the holy silence that follows a bishop's ordination of a priest by
'the laying on of hands'. It is the latter sense that is appropriately
uppermost, because the phrase — like the word *reverence* — belongs
solely to the religious ceremony and permits the romantic interpretation only in the specific context of the poem.

Let me make one other comment on Wain's lexicon in this
poem. He is explicitly writing a love poem but just as explicitly he
is eschewing hyperbole. Bearing in mind the tradition of love poetry
to be couched in elaborately ornate language, he contrasts his own
reaction to love as calling rather for the silence of awe. And although
he technically apologises for this low-key style, he criticises the converse approach by saying that highly-wrought verse is nothing but
glibness. To express this, he risks a conflict of tone by illustrating
glibness through his echo of the catch-phrase cliché, 'all dressed
up and nowhere to go'.

This works, it seems to me, because we get the clear impression that the introduction of this jarring piece of inappropriate
language is deliberate. Unfortunately for the increasing numbers
of those whose use of English is for international purposes, the
type of effect attempted here by Wain tends to be elusive. Even
a *receptive* knowledge of lexicon adequate to evaluating effective
collocations (and noticing miscollocations) is acquired only slowly
and uncertainly. It follows that a *productive* capacity in this respect
is still more difficult to achieve. A proposed newspaper headline

SON KILLS MUM'S LOVER

was itself killed only just in time by a watchful language supervisor
who pointed out, with pardonable sarcasm, that this was no more
appropriate for a suburban domestic calamity than it would have
been as a summary of *Hamlet*. The associations of *Mum* with the
light-hearted love of happy family life precludes its collocation with
words of passion and murder.

A graduate student from abroad, whose general-purpose English was excellent, once wrote me a most courteous letter of thanks for hospitality, and this included the sentence:

> When I was saying cheerio as I begged you to excuse me after lunch, I wished I could express the sublimity and privilege of making the acquaintance of your wife and kids.

The use of *cheerio*, even in speech, would occur only between intimates, and its informality makes it especially unwelcome in the written environment of expressions like 'taking leave' or 'begging to be excused'. As for the slang *kids*, not only does it sadly miscollocate with *acquaintance*, *privilege*, and *sublimity*, but it is a word that natives themselves find hard to use without making other natives feel it is inappropriate. It can occur a little more easily with the possessive *my* than with the possessive *your*, but is in any case less satisfactorily applied to anyone's offspring than to youngsters in general.[1]

For let me make quite clear that appropriacy is acquired slowly and unevenly by us all. Native speakers have particular difficulty not so much through introducing informal expressions as in clumsily avoiding them and thereby showing their unfamiliarity with more formal discourse. Our awareness that split infinitives should be avoided ought to be matched by awareness that the avoidance itself should not be left obvious. Indeed, such incomplete revision is doubly unfortunate in

> The professor intended privately to refute the argument

since it is now unclear whether it refers to a private intention or a private refutation. A letter to *The Times* in London not long ago began: 'How foolish can one become!' It seems likely that the writer had wanted to use that colloquially familiar expression of impatience 'How silly can you get' but felt this was not the kind of thing to write in *The Times*. But instead of totally recasting what was to be said, the writer has mechanically replaced the informal *get*

---

[1]Note the unwelcome stylistic discord of *eyeful* in one of the translations cited on p. 30 above (footnote 1):

> Ning was overjoyed and had a feast prepared. Friends and relatives were invited. When someone wanted to have an eyeful of the bride, Xiaoqian came out in her gorgeous wedding-gown.

by an inappropriate synonym *become* and cobbled together some
other changes in the hope that they would match. Worse, a news
item in the London *Times* on 6 September 1985 used *bacterium*
twice as a singular noun, and one sentence read as follows:

> The bacterium ... are harmless unless they multiply past
> a certain concentration.

Here we have a journalist showing some awareness that the ordinary word *bacteria* is related to a more technical-sounding form
bacterium. He is reporting an outbreak of legionella, so he tries —
ludicrously — to ape the language appropriate to medical science.

The problem for all of us is aggravated by two factors. First,
as we expand our experience and our responsibilities in an ever-
shrinking world and in a world ever more dependent on the passing
of information, we are faced with the need to expand our repertoire
and learn to operate in additional varieties of language. Second,
what constitutes appropriacy changes with time; and throughout
our lives we have to be sensitively alert to these changes and res-
ponsive to their demands. We shall look at some examples of this
in my concluding lectures. To both of these factors we must add
(for English more than most languages) the enormous size of the
vocabulary from which appropriacy items have to be chosen — the
vast majority of them in danger of being imperfectly learned since
they lie well outside that common lexical core I mentioned in my
first lecture.

But let me not exaggerate. As we have considered the various
samples of rather sharply differentiated styles of English, I have
repeatedly drawn attention to grammatical and lexical features by
comparing them with other and more familiar ones. On considering the excerpt on Yeats by Harold Bloom, I pointed out that
instead of a noun clause as subject we might have had the *it*-
construction that would have placed the noun clause at the end.
With reference to the financial jargon in the novel by Thomas, I
said that *order of magnitude* was used 'instead of the less style-specific
word *scale*'. In neither case would the more familiar alternative have
been by an means inappropriate.

In short, beside the relatively marked linguistic features which
in an extreme sense characterise appropriacy, there are relatively neutral expressions which can replace them without descent into positive
inappropriacy. If there is any general tendency in the changing
scene of what constitutes appropriate language, I would say that

it is a movement towards a middle ground in which the language does not obtrusively type-cast the text as belonging to one style rather than another. This is certainly the direction in which the Plain English movement is seeking to influence us. It has much in common with the low key struck by John Wain in his love poem. To put it differently, it is not so much that language that is all dressed up has nowhere to go: it is rather that this is the language that is most liable to go astray.

Lecture Eight
Facing Constraint

When we decide what clothes to put on for a given occasion or purpose (to go shopping, to go jogging, to play golf, teach a class, attend a meeting, go to church, join a friend for lunch), our choice is determined by our sense of appropriacy. There is great scope for personal preference, but we are liable to be adversely (if silently) judged if our choice strays too far from the *general* sense of appropriacy. The linguistic analogue of this was the subject of my seventh lecture.

But there are many situations where the form of dress we wear is not left to our own judgement. In the armed forces, you may be improperly dressed if you have one button of your jacket undone: and for this transgression you can be formally charged and duly punished. In civilian life, penalties are less drastic, though most societies set legal limits on decency in clothing; and if you are indecently dressed, you may find yourself in court. Even without enforcement by military or civil law, a restaurant may demand that a man wear a tie if he wishes to eat there and likewise refuse admission to a woman if she is wearing jeans. An invitation to a formal occasion will usually specify the type of dress to be worn: 'Dinner jacket without decorations' reads a card on one occasion; or 'Doctors in scarlet'; or 'Ladies shall wear hats and gloves'. In Jakarta, 'Dress: Batik' means *long-sleeved* batik. On 25 December 1985, the *Straits Times* published a notice newly posted at the Singapore Turf Club. It read:

> To maintain the image of our Club, only those persons appropriately dressed will be admitted to the Public Stands. Boxer shorts and sleeveless singlets and slippers are not considered appropriate dress.

There are linguistic analogues to these situations too, and it is they that will occupy our attention in this lecture.

As with our discussion of lexical selection in Lecture Seven, it is useful to distinguish *content* matters from *style* matters when we approach the issue of constraints on language use. Constraints governed by legal enactment usually relate to content. Thus we need not concern ourselves here with the constraints imposed through fear of a libel action or breach of a trade description act. Of rather greater interest is the notion of legal copyright and the fact that in consequence pieces of language as short as a brand-name like *Anchor Beer* or as long as a whole book like Golding's *Darkness Visible* are regarded as being in private ownership, to be used only in certain circumstances or with properly certified permission. We are free to read Stoppard's *Travesties* but we are not free to perform it.

Then again, in matters of legal commitment, there are carefully worded formulae to which we are constrained. On getting married, whether in a church or by a civil ceremony, a specific form of words is required from the officiating officer and from the bridal couple: it will not do for a man just to say, 'Yes, I love you, and I'll take good care of you' — though this may be a fairly close paraphrase. In giving evidence in a court of law, a witness is required to affirm or swear to tell 'the truth, the whole truth, and nothing but the truth'. It will not do for a witness just to say, 'Of course, your honour, I shall naturally tell the truth'. Indeed, the built-in redundancy so common in all communication is particularly well justified here. A witness who gave his correct name, address, and age — but the rest of whose evidence was a pack of lies — could truthfully answer 'Yes' if afterwards asked if he had told the truth. Some of his evidence was true, after all. What he had not done was to tell the '*whole* truth' and still less 'nothing but the truth'.

Most societies have laws regulating the kind of extreme language that can be used in certain circumstances: swearing and blasphemy, for example. A law concerning the latter is still on the British Statute Book and was invoked in the 1970s to the applause of some people, the disgust of others, and the astonishment of most, especially as the offending document was a *poem*. There are usually legal constraints upon obscene language (for example, using it in public, over telephone lines, etc), though what actually is deemed an obscenity varies from country to country and from generation to generation.

The fact that public prosecution for linguistic offences is

relatively rare is not to be attributed to laxity on the part of police and other executive authorities: still less to a law-abiding restraint on the part of ordinary citizens. Rather, it is to be attributed to the controls exercised by the media themselves. If a letter to the editor of a newspaper contains coarse or obscene words (usually as so judged by conventions determined by the editor and staff themselves), that letter will not be published, or, if it is, the questionable words will be replaced by innocuous ones or by bashful asterisks. If a journalist writes an article that makes allegations about an individual's behaviour or which seems to make too liberal a use of someone else's writing, the editor will have it looked over by a lawyer to see whether it is likely to be actionable for libel or breach of copyright; and if it is so deemed, the article will not be published. Analogous constraints are exercised by those responsible for broadcasting by radio and television.

Some types of constraint are widely established conventions so that they come close to the concept of appropriacy that we examined in Lecture Seven. Formal meetings of trade unions or university faculties or local authorities or residents' associations will have 'standing orders' which lay down *procedures* for *debate*, for *proposing* a *motion* or an *amendment* to a motion: the very words themselves redolent of firm constraint. One notable feature is that anyone speaking does so technically on the invitation of the person occupying the 'chair' and is obliged to address himself or herself to the chair and to refer to other members present in the third person:

> Madam Chairperson, I really must protest at what Mr Low has just said. Is it not clear to him that other members of this Council have already resolved that no funds be voted for that project in the present financial year?

If that intervention had taken the form that would have been natural in an ordinary discussion, the speaker would have been called to order by the chair:

> Oh, come on, Mr Low. Really! You know perfectly well that the rest of us have decided not to spend money on that this year.

In the British Parliament, such constraints are developed to a high degree: not merely do members of the Commons have to observe the convention of addressing the chair but they must refer to other members in terms of constituency, not using personal names:

> Mr Speaker, I hope I may correct the statement made by the honourable member for Toytown, which he must surely know is quite inaccurate.

Among the many rules of parliamentary language designed to keep debating standards up and tempers down, one is illustrated here: the total proscription of such words as *lie* or *liar* in any comment that a member may make about another.

In the administration of such constraints, the arbiter of propriety is the person occupying the chair, just as with newspapers, it is the editor. To say that exercising this authority is censorship is to put the matter censorially, but that is of course precisely what it is. But the editorial role goes far beyond momentous issues like libel or obscenity. Those who publish newspapers and books require material that they print to follow a 'house style' which regulates usage down to an extraordinary degree of detail such as (indeed especially) spelling and punctuation. Thus even a casual scrutiny of the daily newspapers widely read in Singapore will reveal quite minute differences that are observed with scrupulous regularity. In the *International Herald Tribune* and in the *Asian Wall Street Journal*, for example, abbreviated titles such as 'Mr' and 'Mrs' are always followed by a period, whereas in the *Straits Times* they are not. The former practice is common in American house styles, the latter is common in British house styles. But regulated differences of this kind are by no means always a matter of American versus British practice. Some British houses, for example, spell *connection* with *x*, others with *ct*. Whether or not rules vary from publisher to publisher, however, it must be recognised that a very great deal of the regularity that we find in printed English anywhere in the world is imposed by publishing institutions in this way. And of course, *mutatis mutandis*, something of the sort applies to the electronic media, as for example in the broad standard of pronunciation to be adopted. It is significant, in this connection, to note the terms used for some of the major types of English pronunciation. The fact that we can talk about 'BBC English' or (in the United States) about what is called 'network English' reflects our recognition of the authority exercised by the broadcasting authorities upon their microphone staff.

There is an extreme case of constraint in the usage of air traffic control. The need for speedy understanding with as complete an avoidance of ambiguity as is possible has brought about a quite detailed degree of international agreement regulating, for example, the way individual letters of the alphabet are identified and the names of numerical digits pronounced: obvious desiderata in circumstances where the radio telephony may be far from ideal acoustically but where error is potentially lethal. Thus in ground-to-air or air-to-ground communication, Singapore Airlines Flight SQ 59 will become 'Sierra Quebec fife niner'. Several other numerals similarly require the use of a pronunciation quite literally foreign to English ('thousand' becomes *tousand*, 'three' is *tree*), but such departures are reasonable enough given the need to agree on a pronunciation which will present no difficulty for any non-native speaker (the voiceless fricative *th* is a problem for many) and which will be unambiguous through headphones (again the English *th* presents problems). But it is regulation that matters, not reasonableness. The letter-naming code is open to many obvious criticisms: 'Quebec' must be uttered as *kay*BEK, that is, with no [kw] sound and indeed perhaps suggesting by its most audible syllable that it refers to the letter *b*. Again, the code for *h* is *ho*TEL, though in the pronunciation of many people there is no *h*-sound and in any case the most audible syllable begins with *t*. But no pilot or ground controller is permitted to replace any item in the code with something he personally thinks would be better. Unless and until the code is changed by international agreement, it must be uniformly and universally followed: and rightly so, of course.

During the period that English came to be established as the language of international air navigation, controls over the permitted forms have become very much tighter, in most cases institution-alising linguistic habits developed for military flying by the air forces of Britain and America. The present standard phraseology represents what is probably the most radical and successful piece of linguistic engineering yet performed. It not merely constrains users to a relatively small number of lexical items and grammatical patterns, but the latter are not necessarily even a subset of the grammatical patterns found in ordinary English. For example, if we want to say 'I'm now going to repeat what I've just said', the obligatory expression is 'I say again' — without, it should be noticed, the option of using the progressive or future. The question 'How do you read?' is the sole approved form of an inquiry meaning 'Am

I clear enough?' or 'How well is my voice coming across?' or 'Can you hear me properly?' Instead of 'That's the end of my message', one must just say 'Out'; instead of 'Fine — I've got your message', the correct form is 'Roger'. And many of the most frequently-used phrases are shortened into acronyms; for example *ETA* for 'estimated time of arrival', *CB* for 'cumolo-nimbus' — the thunder clouds which produce hazardous degrees of turbulence.

Here now is a plausible exchange[1] between a Japanese aircraft and Narita International Airport:

> ACFT: Narita Approach — Japanair 403 approaching Choshi 6000 feet
>
> APP : Roger Japanair 403 — leave Choshi heading 319 for Lake — contact Arrival 125.8 — report heading
>
> ACFT: Wilco Narita Approach — heading 319 — changing to 125.8 — Japanair 403
>
> ...
>
> ACFT: Narita Arrival — Japanair 403 established on the localiser
>
> ARR : Japanair 403 — descend on the glide path — maintain not less than 170 knots to outer marker — contact Tower 124.9
>
> ...
>
> ACFT: Narita Tower — Japanair 403 long final
>
> TWR : Japanair 403 — continue approach — one ahead to land — report on four-mile final.
>
> ...
>
> ACFT: Narita Tower — Japanair 403 four-mile final
>
> TWR : Japanair 403 cleared to land — wind 330 degrees 15 knots

I have chosen excerpts that have none of the acronymic technicalities that would be totally opaque to ordinary users of English; but even so, what we have here stands in need of 'translation'. And of course we must remember that if we had heard this instead of reading it, the English would have seemed still more unfamiliar: thus the radio frequency '124.9' would be heard as 'wun too fower

---

[1] Adapted from Leveson and Cass, 1984; cf also Field, 1985.

day-see-mal niner'. But we also have to know that there are several
control authorities at each major airport. 'Narita Approach' is one
such authority; 'Narita Arrival' is another; and the 'Tower' is a third;
and each control passes an aircraft to another with instruction to
make contact by switching to a specific (and of course different)
frequency.

Most messages begin with a vocative and end with a signature.
Thus in the first message here, the aircraft flight deck addresses
the outermost control with the words 'Narita Approach' and goes
on to identify the sender as 'Japanair 403', stating the aircraft's
horizontal position in relation to the Choshi VHF omnidirectional
beacon and giving its vertical position as '6000 feet'. Approach
replies that the message has been received ('Roger') and uses a
vocative to make it quite clear which aircraft is being addressed;
instruction is then given for proceeding beyond the Choshi beacon
as a compass bearing 319. Since it is an established convention
(that is, shared knowledge) that the 360 degrees are counted in a
clockwise direction from north as zero, making due east ninety
degrees, it follows that 319 is approximately north-north-west. The
instruction then goes on to tell the aircraft to switch to a different
control, namely 'Arrival', and the frequency for tuning in. Finally,
control asks the aircraft to confirm that the message has been
correctly received. This the aircraft does by saying the crew 'will
comply' and signing off with the aircraft's identity.

The next excerpt comes at a later stage when the aircraft
tells arrival control that it is now lined up with the runway and
responding to the localiser beam of the instrument landing system.
The pilot is given a minimum speed for the gliding descent and
is handed on to tower control, with a new radio frequency. In due
course, the Japanese pilot calls the tower to report that his aircraft
is now in its final approach more than four nautical miles away.
The tower tells him to report again when he is four miles away
and warns him that there is an aircraft ahead which must land
first. The last call from the tower not only gives permission to land
but provides up-to-the-minute data on wind speed and direction.

Even without going into the carefully specified procedures for
dealing with potential disasters ('May Day' calls) or less serious
emergencies ('pan pan pan' calls), it will be seen that the language
of air navigation imposes a very strict discipline on flying personnel
and ground staff — for which the rest of us must be grateful. Our
lives depend on it. Now, despite the irony that air navigation uses

values like *knots* for speed and *nautical miles* for distance, which are derived from sea navigation, there is the further irony that, for this much older form of mass transportation, standardisation and control of communication are still at a much more rudimentary stage. True, there have long been flag codes, the semaphore signalling system, and Morse transmitted by light pulses and radio pulses. But the first of these is restricted to a few stereotyped messages and the others are little more than alphabets. A generative system of message production has been lacking — along with the will for international agreement about the language on which it should be based.

Developments of the past four or five years have brought us closer to the possibility of a maritime discipline and practice analogous to that in the air. This is now recognised as *necessary* because of the extreme size of such ships as bulk carriers for oil and the existence of many dangerously crowded sea lanes such as the English Channel or the Straits of Malacca. It is recognised as *urgent* in view of the large numbers of mutually incomprehensible languages spoken by bridge personnel and in shore stations throughout the world. And it is recognised as *practicable* now that voiced VHF radio telephony has all but replaced short wave Morse-key transmission for ship-to-ship and ship-to-shore communication.

Thanks to a collaborative project involving two experienced master mariners and two academic applied linguists, a system called *Seaspeak* has been devised.[1] Trials have been carried out in several parts of the world, improvements have been built into the system and now training manuals have been published. Seaspeak is currently working its way through such bodies as the International Maritime Organisation to achieve not merely international approval but international agreement on adoption. In the example that follows, we have the imagined approach to Singapore of a ship called Western Sky:

> WS : Singapore Port Operations, Singapore Port Operations. This is Western Sky Nine-Victor-Alfa-Tango: Western Sky, Nine-Victor-Alfa-Tango. On VHF channel one-two. Over.
>
> SPO: Western Sky, Western Sky. This is Singapore Port Operations. Over.
>
> WS : Singapore Port Operations. This is Western Sky.

---

[1]Cf Weeks *et al.* (1984), from which the exchanges that follow are quoted.

Information: my ETA position: East Johore Pilot
Station is time: one-three-four-five UTC.

SPO: Western Sky. This is Singapore Port Operations.
Mistake. Time is: one-four-three-zero UTC now.
Stay on. Over.

WS : Singapore Port Operations. This is Western Sky.
Correction. My ETA is one-five-four-five UTC.
Over.

SPO: Western Sky. This is Singapore Port Operations.
Information received. Your ETA position: East
Johore Pilot Station is time: one-five-four-five
UTC. Instruction: Anchor in the General Pur-
pose Anchorage. Reason: your berth is occupied.
Please acknowledge anchorage instruction. Over.

In ordinary parlance, Western Sky here informs Singapore that she
expects to be (ETA) at the East Johore Pilot Station by quarter to
two in the afternoon. Singapore replies that this must be wrong
since it is already half-past two. Western Sky then notices that one
digit had been wrong and gives the ETA as quarter to four.

The similarity of Seaspeak conventions to those we have seen
in air navigation will be clear. The addressee is always named first;
there is the well-justified insistence on redundancy through repetition; there is the common use of expressions like ETA; numerical
values are given as sequences of individual digit names (thus 'one-
five-four-five' and not 'fifteen-forty-five'). An important difference
is the appositive use of abstract communication markers followed
by the relevant message:

Instruction: Anchor in the General Purpose Anchorage.

Reason: Your berth is occupied.

We have dealt so far with constraints that are exercised by
authority: by legal statute in the case of such matters as copyright or blasphemy; by an organisation as in the exercise of house
style; by a committee as in the devising of standing orders; by
international agreement as with the administration of aviation
radio-telephony. The motivation behind the adoption of such constraints varies enormously: it may be an obvious need for public
safety; it may be in the interests of clear and fair debate, without
the intrusion of personal abuse; it may be the protection of an
individual's property (as with copyright); it may be merely in the

interests of neatness and consistency, as with the hyphenation rules in a printing-house style.

With the last example we considered, *Seaspeak*, we saw a set of potential constraints with a clear motivation but without as yet an imposing authority. I would like to look now at a somewhat similar situation of constraints that are still largely potential but where the motivation is of a socio-political nature. When I made reference earlier to obscenity and blasphemy, I mentioned that standards change: there can be no absolutes, since what offends the sensibilities in one country or in one generation is accepted without demur in another. In Shakespeare's time, the youthful but vigorously extreme protestant movement was sufficiently influential for legal penalties to be imposed on anyone who broke the Judaeo-Christian commandment about taking 'the Name of the Lord thy God in vain'. Today for most people in Britain, America and other English-speaking countries, the very notion of blasphemy is unfamiliar, let alone the observance of the law which in Britain still technically regulates it.

On the other hand, terms of racial abuse (*nigger*, *wog*, *chink*, *yid*, and the like) are now as rigorously banned as were swear words in earlier generations. The terrible history of racial hatred and the outbreaks of actual genocide within living memory are enough to explain this particular change in human sensibility — and the change is virtually world-wide. What is worth noting in the present context is the clearly perceived relation between verbal behaviour and physical behaviour. The former is not merely a surrogate of the latter; it may lead directly to it. So if it is desirable to improve physical behaviour, it is necessary to improve the linguistic behaviour which refers to it.

So it is with the feminist movement, again a world-wide phenomenon of social sensibility but nowhere as strong as in English-speaking countries. It follows that, as an essential part of the measures required to remove the perceived discrimination against women, the movement insists on the need to observe linguistic rules that will imply the social, political and economic equality of women with men. Let me give some examples of the current linguistic practices to which feminists not surprisingly object. An entertainer (writing, of all places, in the British magazine *Woman*) expresses himself thus:

My ambition is to have ... a family show. People would

bring their wives, mothers and children.

Clearly, this unconsciously assumes that 'people' are male. In the same way, such words as *tenant, resident, citizen, occupier, employee* tend to imply males unless the context specifies otherwise, and so an MP was able to state in a BBC broadcast:

> What causes most distress to the residents is the kerb-crawlers, molesting their women-folk.

Even nationality names will, out of context, connote males only: 'There were two Singaporeans on the plane', 'I saw three Germans jogging near the Embassy'. So it seemed perfectly natural for a journalist of the London *Sunday Times* to write:

> Sharing our railway compartment were two Norwegians and their wives.

We would have been astonished if the article had read:

> Sharing our railway compartment were two Norwegians and their husbands.

It is even more notable that the word *adult* which we might expect to be as inclusive of males and females as any word in the language, can slip into use as equivalent to '*male* adult'. Consider the following quotation from the *New York Times*:[1]

> Another difference ... is that it is strictly an adult group. It does not take in either women or students who are still in High School.

Changing our linguistic habits to replace such male orientation by an explicitly 'inclusionary' one would involve a more fundamental exercise of constraint than any we have considered, since usages challenged include the entire reference base of human beings which has traditionally in English (as in other languages) used masculine forms as unmarkedly inclusive. Thus the word *mankind* refers to all humanity, as does *man* in such expressions as 'Man is mortal'. By contrast, *womankind* could refer only to human females, and equally expressions such as 'Hair is woman's crowning glory'

---

[1] I am indebted for these examples to an article by Jenny Cheshire, which appeared in *English Today*, January 1985.

cannot be taken to refer equally to the hair on male heads. We may further compare and contrast the disciplines of anthropology and gynaecology, the latter relating to women only while the former relates (or should relate) to humanity as a whole — though it is said that a distinguished anthropologist once began a paper with the generalisation:

Man's basic needs are food, shelter, and access to women.

The principle of marked and unmarked pairs is widespread in language, such that the unmarked regularly subsumes the marked but not the converse. Thus it is common for the past tense of verbs to be literally marked (that is, morphologically) in contrast to the present, and in consequence for the present to have a double use: one including all time reference, the other excluding all time reference except the present. The marked tense on the other hand has a more restricted reference. This is why

Penguins live in the Antarctic

is taken to mean not only that they live there now but that they lived there last year too, and are expected to be living there next year as well. By contrast, in

David Lim lived in Jurong

the verb form marks and limits reference to the past alone. Analogously, the existence of such pairs as *man – woman, male – female, host – hostess* indicates our propensity to regard the latter in each case as the marked special case of the former. It is significant that there are such derived verbs as *man* enabling us to say that 'The yacht was *manned* by a crew of four: my son and his wife plus his brother and sister'. And I could ask a woman colleague if she would *host* a party. But there is, I think, no verb to *woman* or to *hostess*, and if there were, the subject could not be male.

I mention these well-known facts as a reminder of how deep-seated are the built-in linguistic constraints that the feminist movement seeks to replace by others. Yet despite the formidable nature of the challenge, the movement has made impressive headway. This is especially so in the United States where numerous legislative enactments have been passed and implemented. In the United Kingdom, successes have been more modest but are nonetheless significant. Business organisations have proscribed what are called 'sexist' forms in their notices and correspondence, and trade unions have been similarly active. For example, in May 1984 the council of the Association of University Teachers adopted a resolution instructing the Executive Committee

> to ensure that all future documents exclude the use of
> gender specific terms (e.g. man, he) where what is in-
> tended is reference to both genders.

In consequence, the AUT issued a note of guidance to all branches detailing what it called 'unacceptable usage' along with the corresponding 'good usage'. For example, *manpower* should be replaced by *work-force*; *man-made* by *artificial*; *chairman* by *chairperson*[1] or *convenor*; *girl* by *woman* (cf the discussion of 'Brook Street girl' in Lecture One); *yours fraternally* by *yours in comradeship*. The document concluded by listing items that 'should be avoided altogether', an example being the adjective *manly*.

In consequence, there are few of us indeed who do not already experience constraint upon our usage in this sensitive area. Certainly the Christian Church is not exempted. In 1983, an organisation called One for Christian Renewal issued a booklet which by its punning title 'Bad Language in Church' confirms the point I made earlier that the informal term traditionally applied to swearing and obscenity must now be applied to a quite different type of offence. Bad language in this context is male-oriented language. If *girl* and *man-made* seem repellent to feminists in the trade unions, concepts like *the Son of Man* and God *the Father* made incarnate in God *the Son* are inevitably no less objectionable to feminists in the Church. Just after the booklet was published, a leading article in the London *Times* (8 October 1983) was devoted to this issue, protesting that 'there is something artificial and clumsy about trying to use the English language to make an ideological point'. Since the feminist case rests precisely on the claim that the English language has already been used to make just such an ideological point — but a male-oriented one — the *Times* leader-writer is on shaky ground here. But he (surely not she?) is somewhat more persuasive in his concluding paragraph:

> The purging of the language of all metaphors with
> a gender connotation would be an impoverishment,

---

[1]Some people urge a distinction between *-person* for the office and *-man/-woman* for a specific occupant.

> and a particular impoverishment in religious liturgy ...
> There really is no insult to women in using for the
> First Person of the Christian Trinity the hallowed ex-
> pression 'Almighty Father', and only a peculiar type of
> single-mindedness would see it as such.

A stream of letters from *Times* readers demonstrated that such single-mindedness is not all that peculiar — at any rate if we take *peculiar* in the sense of 'rare', 'unusual'. One letter, from the Chairperson and Vice-Chairperson of the Christian Renewal Organisation, went so far as to say that such expressions as *God the Father* were 'to the detriment of God's femininity'.

If those who are battling for a consciously engineered 'inclu-sionary' (i.e. non-sexist) language are thus willing to see theology itself re-thought, the battle is serious indeed. It is true, of course, as the *Times* leader-writer noted, that inclusionary language is some-what 'artificial and clumsy'. The following dictionary definition of the term *sub-lease* actually survived to the stage of printed proofs before being abandoned:

> an agreement by which someone who rents a property
> from its owner themself rents the property to someone
> else.

But we may be sure that the revised version will not assume that all individuals involved in subleasing are male. The constraints are in operation: only the devices of implementation are yet to be settled, and these include some very 'artificial' devices indeed — such as the numerous proposals for a sex-neutral singular pronoun which have included *co, e, hesh, hir,* and one much earlier inven-tion, the nineteenth-century *thon*. Commenting with some asperity on this last, William Zinsser remarked (*Writing Well*, New York: Harper and Row, 1980):

> Maybe I don't speak for the average American, but I
> very much doubt if thon wants that word in thons
> language or that thon would use it thonself. This is not
> how the language changes.

Well, Zinsser is broadly right; but as we have seen with the language of air navigation, if the constraints are sufficiently well-motivated, artificiality such as *niner* and *tousand*, or clumsiness such as heavy repetition, can readily be tolerated. Already the form *s/he* has some modest currency in writing. And who would have predicted a dozen years ago that the option of using the feminine title *Ms* would be provided on immigration forms around the world?

I said in my first lecture that the 'most abiding difficulty about human communication is that it is human', but that while this means that every communication is subject to human frailty (and the prejudices, predispositions, failures of perspectives, imagination and sympathy to which our individual character or cultural background has condemned us), there is a brighter side. Human communication is human too in its potentiality for creativity, for responsiveness to change, and to the demands of new conditions, new environments, new challenges.

We have seen in these lectures something of the ways in which successful texts built on such human propensities as the willingness to co-operate, the willingness to believe, the willingness to look for meaning. We have seen something of the ways in which the sympathetic communicator seeks out in the addressee the area of shared knowledge, is careful to provide an orientation in space and time, to use the lexical and grammatical resources of language to distribute information in the optimal order for access by the addressee; to express it in forms appropriate to the medium and the occasion; and to be sensitive to the insecurities and the perceived injustices that the addressee may feel.

Bibliography

Chafe, W. 'Givenness, Contrastiveness, Definiteness, Subjects, Topics, and Point of View', pp. 25–55 of Li, 1976.

Cole, P. and J.L. Morgan. *Syntax and Semantics 3: Speech Acts* (New York: Academic Press, 1975).

Cooper, C.R. and S. Greenbaum. *Studying Writing: Linguistic Approaches* (Beverly Hills: Sage, 1986).

Crystal, D. 'Neglected Grammatical Factors in Conversational English', pp. 153–66 of Greenbaum *et al.*, 1980.

de Beaugrande, R. *Text, Discourse, and Process* (London: Longman, 1980).

_____. *Text Production: Toward a Science of Composition* (Norwood, NJ: Ablex, 1984).

Eco, U. *Reflections on the Name of the Rose* (London: Secker and Warburg, 1984).

Edmondson, W. *Spoken Discourse* (London: Longman, 1981).

Enkvist, N.E. 'Marked Focus: Functions and Constraints', pp. 134–52 of Greenbaum *et al.*, 1980.

_____. *Impromptu Speech: A Symposium* (Åbo: Åbo Akademi, 1982).

_____. 'Text Linguistics for the Applier: An Orientation', in U. Connor and R.P. Kaplan, *Analysis of Writing: Models and Methods* (Reading, Mass.: Addison-Wesley, 1986).

Field, A. *International Air Traffic Control* (Oxford: Pergamon, 1985).

Firbas, J. 'A Functional View of "Ordo Naturalis"', *Brno Studies in English* 13(1979): 29–59.

_____. 'On the Dynamics of Written Communication in the Light of the Theory of Functional Sentence Perspective', pp. 40–71 of Cooper and Greenbaum, 1986.

Greenbaum, S., G. Leech and J. Svartvik. *Studies in English Linguistics* (London: Longman, 1980).

Grice, H.P. 'Logic and Conversation', pp. 41–58 of Cole and Morgan, 1975.

Grimes, J.E. *The Thread of Discourse* (The Hague: Mouton, 1975).

Haegeman, L. 'Pragmatic Conditionals in English', *Folia Linguistica* 18(1984): 485–502.

Haiman, J. 'The Iconicity of Grammar', *Language* 56 (1980): 515–40.

Halliday, M.A.K. *Language as Social Semiotic* (London: Arnold, 1978).

_____. *An Introduction to Functional Grammar* (London: Arnold, 1985).

Hoey, M.P. *On the Surface of Discourse* (London: Allen and Unwin, 1983).

Jordan, M.P. *Rhetoric of Everyday English Texts* (London: Allen and Unwin, 1984).

Leech, G.N. and M.H. Short. *Style in Fiction* (London: Longman, 1981).

Leech, G.N. *Principles of Pragmatics* (London: Longman, 1983).

Leveson, L.F. and M. Cass. *Skytalk: English for Air Communication* (Cheltenham: Thornes, 1984).

Li, C.N. *Subject and Topic* (New York: Academic Press, 1976).

Lyons, J. *Semantics* (Cambridge: University Press, 1977).

Nash, W. *Designs in Prose* (London: Longman, 1980).

_____. *The Language of Humour* (London: Longman, 1985).

Quirk, R. *Style and Communication in the English Language* (London: Arnold, 1982).

Quirk, R., S. Greenbaum, G. Leech and J. Svartvik. *A Comprehensive Grammar of the English Language* (London: Longman, 1985).

Schenkein, J. *Studies in the Organisation of Conversational Interaction* (New York: Academic Press, 1978).

Searle, J.R. *Expression and Meaning* (Cambridge: University Press, 1979).

Sinclair, J.McH. 'Discourse in Relation to Language Structure and Semiotics', pp. 110–24 of Greenbaum *et al.*, 1980.

Sinclair, J.McH. and D. Brazil. *Teacher Talk* (Oxford: University Press, 1982).

Svartvik, J. '*Well* in Conversation', pp. 167–77 of Greenbaum *et al.*, 1980.

Taglicht, J. *Message and Emphasis* (London: Longman, 1984).

van Dijk, T.A. *Text and Context* (London: Longman, 1977).

Weeks, F., A. Glover, P. Strevens and E. Johnson. *Seaspeak Reference Manual* (Oxford: Pergamon, 1984).

Widdowson, H.G. *Explorations in Applied Linguistics* (Oxford: University Press, 1984).

Winter, E.O. *Towards a Contextual Grammar of English* (London: Allen and Unwin, 1982).